ENFORCER
TO
ENTREPRENEUR

JERRY ROLLINS

Achieving Hockey Stick Growth
in Life, Business, and Sports

ENFORCER
TO
ENTREPRENEUR

Published and distributed by Merack Publishing.

Library of Congress Control Number: 2020914994

Rollins, Jerry

Enforcer to Entrepreneur: Achieving Hockey Stick Growth In Life, Business, and Sports

ISBN 978-1-949635-51-5 Perfect Bound
ISBN 978-1-949635-53-9 Hardcover
ISBN 978-1-949635-52-2 Ebook

Cover and Interior by Yvonne Parks

DEDICATION

Terrie, when we met I was considered successful to the outside world. However, inside there was something missing that did not allow me to be fulfilled. I did not know it at the time, but it was you.

CONTENTS

FOREWORD
by Stan Fischler

Al Rollins was one of my all-time favorite National Hockey League goaltenders. I first saw him play during the 1944-45 season while attending hockey games with my dad. I was about eleven, and Al quickly became one of my heroes. I never imagined that fifteen years later at the beginning of my six-decade writing career, I'd actually meet him.

He was tall, angular and had a Hollywood look about him.

Every one of his stand-up saves was a work of art.

Plus, he was a champ.

Al helped the 1950-51 Toronto Maple Leafs win the Stanley Cup, and the Vezina Trophy (Best Goalie). Several years later in 1954 he won the Hart Trophy (MVP) with the last-place Chicago Blackhawks.

I followed Ally's—that was his New York nickname—Broadway career from the early 1940s when he played for the New York Rovers to the early 1960s in the twilight of his career with the NHL's New York Rangers.

By the time we met, Al was a Ranger and I was interviewing him for a New York Journal-American newspaper article.(I've since included Al in several of my over one hundred books about hockey, including, *Who's Who in Hockey* and *The Handy Hockey Answer Book*.)

One night, while dining with Al—I couldn't believe I was across the table from my hero—I kept wondering whether there ever would be another Rollins quite like Big Al.

It took awhile for me to get my answer—a half-century if you want to count—but I did. And he just happens to be the author of this book. We were introduced by a hockey historian who'd sent Jerry another article I'd written about his dad. We became friends while bonding over our mutual admiration for Al.

Jerry Rollins may never have played for a Stanley Cup-winner nor won trophies like his dad, but he has emerged a champion in his own right.

But not as a hockey player.

Yeah, Jerry was a pro stickhandler—an impressive feat in itself—but he was smart enough to get out of the puck business when the time was right. And here's where he trod along Champions Boulevard.

Faster than you can say *Wayne Gretzky*, the young Rollins seamlessly moved into the business world running not one, two or three—but five companies.

"I was always amazed at the parallels between successful athletes, business people and business/sports teams," Jerry told me.

Over the past decade, Rollins has coached, counseled and otherwise advised hundreds of CEOs. And that's just for starters.

In addition, Jerry has mentored corporate presidents and business owners—not to mention college and high school students.

How does he reply to them when they call for assistance? The Rollins Game Plan goes like this:

1. I've experienced that issue multiple times and here's the *action plan* that I'd take in addressing the issue.

2. I have a *process* to address the issue that I've refined over the past four decades and will send it to you.

3. There's a *book* with a specific section that can help you and I'll send you a link.

4. There's a *person/resource* you need to connect with, and I'll help you make that connection.

This book should become the bible for any CEO who wants to take his business game higher than it happens to be now.

Not that it should be limited to CEOs.

Jerry Rollins states, "My targets include entrepreneurs who wish to avoid making mistakes that we all make along the way. And that includes mature private businesses that are stuck and looking for some direction."

Who else should read this gem of business literature?

Personally, I'd recommend it for high school, college or university students and pro athletes who are smart enough to look a year or more over their horizons.

To put it succinctly, Jerry knows the score. He's a winner just like my other favorite Rollins named Al.

From champ to champ; like father, like son.

Jerry's landmark work underlines my point.

STAN FISCHLER
Author of one hundred books, newspaper journalist, hockey historian, broadcaster and professor, El Rom, Israel, 2019

INTRODUCTION

The Student Becomes the Teacher

My professional career began as a Major League hockey "enforcer"—a team's tough guy. Now, I coach hundreds of entrepreneurs and CEOs—with revenue ranging from $1 million to $3 billion companies and MBAs from prestigious universities—how to improve their businesses. Not bad for a high school dropout who made two game-changing, life-altering moves:

1. Studying extraordinary people to learn how they became the best in their fields.

2. Writing down all their invaluable advice and insight throughout my own journey to the top.

I also recorded every stage of my progress, including the mistakes, level of commitment and more, as I applied the techniques I learned from those elite business leaders. *Enforcer to Entrepreneur: Achieving Hockey Stick Growth in Life, Business and Sports* is the foolproof playbook I created from that collection of proven strategies.

What do I know?

I know there's a process for everything. Nothing in business is mysterious or elusive and— as I discovered during my hockey career—most everything can be learned. When I started playing hockey, I didn't have the exceptional skills or talent that it took to make it to the pros. So instead, I mimicked and practiced the behaviors and acquired the mindset of the greatest players until I reached my goal. I followed the same course of action in the corporate world. Emulating and using lessons from industry leaders enabled me to not only experience success beyond my wildest dreams, but also show others how to succeed beyond theirs. Anyone can learn to be a success.

What's in it for You?

A whopping 82% of businesses fail due to issues with cash flow, a crucial yet elementary business fundamental. That's why throughout the book, I divulge preventative measures and systems used by the business elite to secure capital, avoid negative cash flow and overcome other occupational pitfalls.

There's also expert counsel for owners and CEOs who have met their financial goals, yet find themselves asking, *"Now what?"* It happened to me, as I explain in chapter ten, *The Stages of Success.*

The chapter includes candid tips to help readers define success, work toward purpose, and move from success to significance. Part of my significance is giving back in the form of this book. I want to help others achieve more and profit from my trials and triumphs.

How do I know?

I believe I was predestined to write this book since my research began organically as a child. Watching my original mentor and NHL star, my dad Al Rollins, along with other remarkable athletes we knew—such as Gordie Howe, Bobby Hull and Wayne Gretzky—I saw what it took to achieve excellence and be an exceptional athlete and team member. I did the same in my second career, except I sought out sales leaders, joined peer groups and kept my eye on the brightest minds in business— the mentors who set the bar for their domains. I saw what they did well, patterned myself after them, then outworked them until I surpassed them.

Why my book?

I share practices that in the past have only been available to captains of industry. Decades of pooled experience that isn't taught in school—even the Ivy League ones. Real stories about real companies with real challenges, and key concepts that withstand the test of time.

I'll never forget fellow Canadian and renowned sales trainer Brian Tracy's parting words at a seminar I attended. He told his audience of thousands that *only 1%* of them would apply something they heard that day—the rest will do nothing. At twenty-six years old, I knew right then that I was in the 1% that would make things happen. His assertion prompted me to start writing down everything I wanted to accomplish, and that process paved my path to business success.

Now, I'm hoping to influence the 1% that will utilize ideas in this book. My goal is for readers to take away ten tangible, actionable things that can be done right now to advance the way they do business. The ten may be different for each reader, but everyone should be able to execute at least ten. (A convenient fill-in chart in the back of the book helps readers keep track of the processes they want to employ.)

Why now?

The compiled advice from predecessors who have been there, and done it best, are in ONE comprehensive book—and in your hands. Unlike other business books that are often too confusing and in-depth for mere mortals to translate into action, *Enforcer to Entrepreneur* delivers in straightforward, unpretentious language.

How soon is too soon to see productivity soar and profits increase? Or, to analyze current company practices and implement new management and leadership methods that achieve maximum potential? To make changes that'll make a difference *now*?

For a guy who didn't have a high school diploma, gaining knowledge from business pioneers was my MBA and the quickest way to the executive suite. I invite you to use what took me years to understand from countless mentors already reaping the multi-million-dollar rewards of big business. This is the book I wish I had starting out. Hope you enjoy it.

Jerry Rollins

CHAPTER 1

My Story: A Tale of Two Careers

The Home Team

When reflecting on my life so far, I can't help but imagine it with an invisible line naturally dividing the milestones and lessons into two parts: life as a professional athlete *before* embarking on a business career and life after, my journey to becoming a CEO through to the present. Dual paths with one common theme woven throughout: team, as in teamwork, teammates and all things teams—cultivating and nurturing great ones. My first team, my family, is where I'll begin my story.

Born in a suburb of Vancouver, British Columbia, I share a birth place with comedian Jim Carrey, cosmetic Botox and the egg carton (really... Google it!). The Rollins kids were raised in a house where competitive sports reigned supreme. My mom, Bertha (a constant presence on the sidelines and in the bleachers) cheered for us while we participated in baseball, wrestling, hockey, football, rugby, volleyball, gymnastics and even table tennis death matches at home.

I learned to skate at age two, a feat not particularly remarkable or uncommon among Canadian boys who grew up in a country where ice hockey was more like a religion than a sport. What was unique was the world-class sports star who taught me to skate, my dad, Al Rollins. A goaltender for the Chicago Blackhawks, New York Rangers and the Toronto Maple Leafs during his spectacular ten-year NHL career in the 1950s, my dad won the triple crown of pro hockey awards—the Stanley Cup, the Vezina Trophy and the Hart Trophy. His sports legacy lives on in displays at Canada's NHL Sports Hall of Fame and as a Saskatchewan Sports Hall of Fame inductee. It's not an exaggeration to say that uncompromising competition is in my DNA.

I went through my formative years thinking that all kids got to hang out in locker rooms with the children of other coaches and professional athletes (including hockey Hall of Famers). These men I considered to be pseudo-uncles and godfathers. In fact, it wasn't until age thirteen when I figured out that my father, too, was a famous, recognizable hometown hero, and why *"the son of Al Rollins"* often preceded my name.

By the time I turned six, my dad's professional playing career ended and he started coaching. Hockey was his identity, and becoming a coach allowed him to stay in the game. His coaching career continued for many years with jobs in Calgary, Spokane, Salt Lake City, Houston, Tulsa and Phoenix.

School Gets Iced out

In my teen years making money became especially important to me and I took on many part-time jobs. These included delivering newspapers, working in construction, bagging groceries and even selling women's jeans (that was a great job!). Because I was working so much, school took second place.

Although I'd found stability in sports and supportive coaches and great male role models (like Mr. Shalley, Mr. Springenatic, Mr. Wells. Mr. Atamanchuk and Mr. Sturko—who took me under their wings at this unsettling time) school took a back seat. During my junior year of high school, I'd already skipped about one hundred days when my mom caught on and issued me an ultimatum. I had three choices:

1. Commit to school.
2. Get a full-time job.
3. Try out for the Western Canada Hockey League (WCHL), a Major Junior league known today as the Western Hockey League.

The hometown WCHL New Westminster Bruins drafted me at sixteen, but training camp just didn't interest me at the time. Since school was never my thing (see: missing one hundred days) and I didn't want to give up sports altogether, I chose door number three, and entered into a hockey career by default.

At seventeen, I got a ten-game tryout with the Flin Flon Bombers. Based in Flin Flon, a small mining community in the northern part of the Canadian province of Manitoba, the

Bombers were one of the top, and toughest, junior teams. If I made the team, I'd be able to work part-time in the copper and zinc mines for a lot more money than I could ever earn stocking shelves somewhere back home. So, I left high school in my junior year for the best of both worlds—playing sports and making money.

In my first tryout game, this huge, tough guy skated behind our net, so I knocked him down. Not used to being knocked down, the guy dropped his gloves. We fought and I held my own, getting in some good shots before the refs broke it up. On the way to the penalty box, he came after me again and I matched him blow-for-blow before the two of us got tossed from the game.

In the locker room after the game, Bombers coach Pat "Paddy" Ginnell—a western Canadian league legend who ruled by fear—welcomed me to the team. The huge, hard-hitting guy I'd tangled with turned out to be future NHL Hall of Famer Clark Gillies. Almost forty years later, he still ranks in the top ten toughest players in NHL history—and I can attest to that fact. Good thing I didn't know who he was, or how feared he'd been, before I fought him.

Fighting for My Identity

Acclimating to Flin Flon's population of 8,000 (compared to the million-plus people in Vancouver) and eight-month long winters weren't the only adjustments I had to make. Living and playing hockey with mostly older guys proved to be a time of tremendous emotional growth for me. Boys turned into men working inside the mines and shoveling snow outside of them in brutal, below-zero temperatures. I acquired a great deal of respect for the locals who spent the majority of their lives toiling a mile underground.

When in town, the players worked in the mornings, then went to practice in the afternoons. We played a seventy-game schedule and spent half the time on a bus traveling to challenge teams spread across four provinces. The extensive travel was the reason so many more WCHL players were drafted to play pro compared to the other two leagues (Ontario and Quebec) which traveled minimally within only one province.

In the requisite exit interview after my first year of juniors, Paddy reminded me that I'd been merely a stopgap to fill a void on the roster. If my skills didn't improve I wouldn't make next year's team. I returned home, got a construction job and played hockey, practicing my skills every night for five months. By my second training camp of junior hockey, I was a top four defenseman on the team and named most improved player by the press. I'd figured out what I was good at and applied it. I wasn't the most talented player, but I discovered that being the tough guy was my chance to make it not only in juniors, but also later in the pros.

That's how I became the enforcer on a hockey team. Enforcers police bad behavior from the other teams' tough guys and protect smaller, more skilled offensive teammates. The role also includes changing the game's tempo when needed. For example, interrupting the other team's hot streak by provoking a fight that forces a whistle and stoppage of play by the ref. I'll admit, it was a scary proposition as a teen to get beat up every day by older guys in front of thousands of people, but that's how I earned my place.

During my last year of juniors (which I wrapped up playing for the Winnipeg Clubs) I'd set a WCHL/WHL record (which has since been broken) for 910 career penalty minutes and 473 single-season penalty minutes in 1974-75. That's when scouts and agents started approaching me about turning pro. I'd found my way into the big leagues.

The Big Leagues

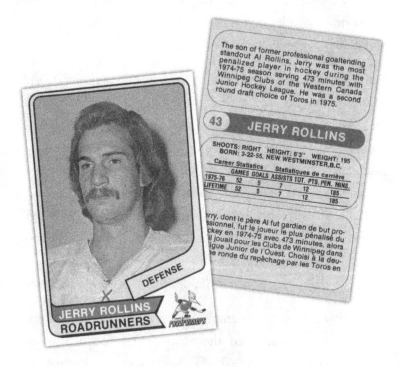

The son of former professional goaltending standout Al Rollins, Jerry was the most penalized player in hockey during the 1974-75 season serving 473 minutes with Winnipeg Clubs of the Western Canada Junior Hockey League. He was a second round draft choice of Toros in 1975.

43   **JERRY ROLLINS**

SHOOTS: RIGHT   HEIGHT: 6'3"   WEIGHT: 195
BORN: 3-22-55, NEW WESTMINSTER, B.C.

Career Statistics		Statistiques de carrière				
	GAMES	GOALS	ASSISTS	TOT.	PTS.	PEN. MINS.
1975-76	52	5	7	12		
LIFETIME	52	5	7	12		185
						185

...rry, dont le père Al fut gardien de but pro-
...ssionnel, fut le joueur le plus pénalisé du
...ckey en 1974-75 avec 473 minutes, alors
...il jouait pour les Clubs de Winnipeg dans
...igue Junior de l'Ouest. Choisi à la deu-
...e ronde du repêchage par les Toros en

DEFENSE

JERRY ROLLINS
ROADRUNNERS

In 1975, fresh from juniors, I ranked as one of the top twenty-six amateur players in the world. At the time and throughout my entire hockey career, there were two competing professional hockey leagues, the National Hockey League (NHL) and the

World Hockey Association (WHA). That fact made it possible for me to be drafted twenty-third by the NHL's Detroit Red Wings *and* twenty-sixth by the WHA's Toronto Toros.

Still, everything comes down to timing and in the 1970s, teams in both leagues were going out of business. Expansion occurred too quickly and there was no due diligence for owners—if they could make the down payments, they were in. Additionally, the NHL and WHA often competed for players, igniting a price war and bidding frenzy, which drove up salaries too high for many owners to sustain. In fact, within the next four years, three of the teams I played for folded while I was on their rosters. That seldom happens these days. During what could be called *the decade of two leagues*, my salary topped out at $75,000, which ranked in the top quarter of compensation for that time. My signing bonus was $50,000. My father, who had an exceptional career only twenty years earlier, earned $15,000 annually at his peak.)

Ultimately it came down to money, and I signed my first of three, three-year contracts with the higher-bidding Toros, making the squad as a rookie. After one year, the team relocated to Birmingham, Alabama, becoming the Birmingham Bulls and the first Major League Hockey team in the state. I'd played only eight games in Birmingham when the financially-strapped owner could no longer afford the balance of my signing bonus and traded me to the Phoenix Roadrunners. Although my stint in Birmingham may have been irrefutably short-lived, it also proved profoundly meaningful. Toronto/Birmingham teammate, and future two-time Stanley Cup winner, Mark Napier helped set me up on a blind date with his girlfriend's best friend, Terrie, who became my future wife. *Spoiler alert:* The Bulls went out of business when the two leagues merged a few years later.

So, Phoenix assumed my contract... that is until the team folded after my first season.

After Phoenix, the Detroit Red Wings signed me to my second three-year contract. At the end of camp, I reported to the Kalamazoo Wings in the International Hockey League (IHL), a team in Detroit's minor system. Next, I played for the Toledo Goaldiggers (also in the IHL), and the Philadelphia Firebirds in the American Hockey League (AHL), which became the third and final Detroit affiliate team I joined that year.

I negotiated a contract buy-out with the Red Wings before the fourth year of my nomadic hockey career, and then signed with the WHA's Indianapolis Racers. That contract would be the last of my three-year contracts. Indianapolis is where I played with the Great One himself, Wayne Gretzky, and future six-time Stanley Cup winner Mark Messier.

My time in Indianapolis was all positive—until the team folded five months later. One day I'm living a hockey player's dream competing in the pros alongside some of the best athletes in the world and the next, the owner tells me he just doesn't want to sell another painting to save the team from bankruptcy. That's exactly the way it happened for me and my teammates on the Racers, the last Major League team I played for.

Wayne's contract was bought by the Oilers, but many guys were casualties of yet another franchise going under. When Indianapolis folded, I was sporting a hip-to-ankle cast for a torn knee ligament, which didn't exactly make me a marketable commodity. Still, the San Diego Hawks, a minor league team in the Pacific Hockey League (PHL), offered me a four-month contract. Within a few weeks, my cast came off and I was able to finish out the year in beautiful San Diego.

Note: Needless to say, things have changed since I played and teams were folding all around me. After the NHL salary cap was instituted in the 2005-06 season following the 2004–05 lockout, the economics of being profitable became easier to manage, thanks in part to lucrative TV contracts. Today, franchises stick with leadership and don't kowtow to the whims of owners. It's good to see more stability coming to the sport.

Early Superpowers of a Future Superstar

I had the honor to be among Wayne Gretzky's first professional teammates on the Indianapolis Racers. I enjoyed an up-close and personal view of a seventeen-year-old Wayne in his fourth pro game, scoring his first Major League goal against the Edmonton Oilers—and his second goal thirty-four seconds later in the same shift. Young Wayne was thoughtful, polite, articulate and like most teens, dealing with his share of acne. I remember him driving to the rink in a Pontiac Trans Am and having to leave early to attend high school.

During one of the first team practices, the coach wanted to see how the legend-in-progress would respond to being checked. He instructed me to do the honors without hurting him. For the entire practice I chased the rookie around, but every time I went to hit him he virtually evaporated. After practice I told the coach I'd be happy to defend Wayne—and if anyone should actually catch him, I'd take care of it.

Career #1: The Goon Old Days

YEAR	TEAM	LEAGUE	GP	G	A	PTS	PIM**
1972-73	Flin Flon Bombers	WCHL	32	0	3	3	99
1973-74	Flin Flon Bombers	WCHL	64	4	12	16	338
1974-75	Flin Flon Bombers	WCHL	9	1	4	5	72
1974-75	Winnipeg Clubs	WCHL	53	6	17	23	401
1975-76	Toronto Toros	WHA	52	5	7	12	185
1976-77	Birmingham Bulls (folded)	WHA	8	0	0	0	17
1976-77	Phoenix Roadrunners (folded)	WHA	63	4	10	14	169
1977-78	Kalamazoo Wings*	IHL	12	0	1	1	68
1977-78	Toledo Goaldiggers*	IHL	16	3	4	7	131
1977-78	Philadelphia Firebirds*	AHL	29	2	2	4	73
1978-79	Indianapolis Racers (folded)	WHA	7	0	1	1	7
1978-79	San Diego Hawks (folded)	PHL	39	2	9	11	145

** From 1972-1979, I was one of the most penalized players in organized amateur and professional hockey with 1,705 penalty minutes and over one hundred fighting majors.

* in Detroit's minor system

Now What?

After San Diego, I still had two years remaining on a three-year guaranteed contract from the WHA and there was a possibility it might be bought by Edmonton. Nonetheless, there weren't any guarantees that Edmonton would even survive at that time and if they did, I wasn't exactly the most gifted player looking to play. Besides that, the unnerving inability to control my own destiny and being beholden to fickle owners who could suddenly uproot my life or life's circumstances, may have scared the hockey out of me for good. Had I gone to college I would have known more about business and understood finances and I would have asked for team financial statements before signing on with an organization.

Like me, most pro athletes see the endgame as making it to the big leagues. We're so focused on our current position that we don't think about how abruptly all of it could disappear. The reality is that most athletic careers end prematurely, leaving many young men and women without plans for their future. Worse off perhaps are the players who have had lengthy careers, but didn't manage their money well, and find themselves in their thirties, out of work with severely limited options. The smart ones got some education or learned a business unrelated to hockey during their off-seasons, so things were in place when their playing days ended. Regrettably, I wasn't among them.

To compound an already challenging situation is the emotional element of the humbling transition. Ex-pro athletes, once renowned and revered—especially with far-reaching TV exposure—suddenly find themselves in a new industry where their plus-minus stats and previously large salaries don't matter. Their egos, along with their celebrity status, nosedive. Suddenly, they're having to prove themselves all over again to their families, to the people they work for and especially to themselves. They're beginning from ground zero like anyone else entering the workforce.

That's why many former athletes look for ancillary positions in the industry—such as coaching, managing or public relations— as a way to stay around the game in some way—*any* way. I would have considered coaching, but I knew I'd simply be trading one financial seesaw for another because coaching roles were just as insecure as being a player. I watched the toll my dad's job took on his life and health with the insecurity of choosing a career in professional coaching. I also knew former teammates who went into coaching and coped with changing teams frequently and continuously starting over. Sometimes, the stats don't even matter and successful coaches find themselves moving on too.

I'd already grown tired of the transient lifestyle after moving to ten cities in seven years. More than ever, after falling in love with Terrie, I craved stability and job security. I wanted to put roots down, find a place to live and a new career—preferably one where I wasn't getting the crap beaten out of me regularly. Terrie and I were ready for the proverbial normal life.

Getting Down to Business

The year was 1979 and as my hockey career came to an end, the NHL voted to absorb the four surviving WHA teams and the

WHA ended, too. Terrie and I chose to stay in San Diego—not exactly the hockey center of the world. Had we moved back to Canada, my name might have provided me with more job opportunities, but we chose Southern California where the athletes were surfers, not hockey players, and ice was never in the forecast. (We're still there 43 years later.)

Once we settled on where to live, I began my own transition to the great unknown, as an unknown myself. Just prior to the NHL/WHA merger, I'd finally negotiated an NHL buy-out of my remaining contract with Indianapolis. With a two-year payout, Terrie and I were able to buy our first house and support ourselves while we both began careers. College wasn't an option for me then because I hadn't finished high school and couldn't spare the time. I needed to make a living and begin again at almost twenty-five—several steps behind my peers with degrees.

So, what kind of business does a high school dropout and former enforcer go into? He goes into sales. I believed that anyone who could generate revenue (I learned that goal scorers in hockey were always secure, and the most highly compensated) will consistently have some level of security in life. Still, entering the business world was like entering another dimension. A dimension where even words such as boards, checks, goals and overtime took on new meanings. I felt intimidated like that insecure kid starting out on his own in Flin Flon again. No, that's not true. It felt even *more* daunting because when I started in juniors, at least I'd played hockey before. I didn't know anything about business or sales.

Lucky for me, I landed my first non-hockey position at a good company with amazing leaders and team members. Unfortunately, I still had a rough time adapting. I faced lots of rejection, took it personally and doubted myself. In fact, 90 days into the new job I told Terrie it was probably time for me to consider other options or to go back to playing hockey.

Even more fortunate than having a great first company was having a smart and supportive wife who wasted no time reminding me that (my) old habits die hard. Despite not having the talent or skills other players did, I still got to the Major Leagues with hard work, focus and dedication (thanks, Mom!). Terrie recommended I trust in my abilities and lean into those same strengths in business too. She punctuated my wake-up call by assuring me she'd love and support me no matter what I did. Quitting too soon could lead to a pattern of job-hopping which is not uncommon among former athletes. That's what you'd call a turning point for me.

Quitting wasn't an option. My hockey experience taught me about grit and dedication, and that challenges and obstacles are often gateways for big opportunities. In fact, many of the fundamental concepts I acquired from sports helped me attain a successful business career, such as:

- Cultivate great mentors.
- Most everything can be learned.

- Use a playbook; develop a plan by utilizing the best practices of successful people.

- Be a team player.

- Outwork the competition.

- Make attaining goals a game.

- Keep score of everything.

- Face your fears and work through them.

- Control your own destiny; building something for others makes *them* wealthy.

- Keep learning; maintaining a high level of performance is harder than achieving it.

So, not having a degree to fall back on, I decided to learn from people who did and were already succeeding in business. I sought out mentors, along with books—some decades old, but still relevant today—and any resources I could get my hands on. I then refocused and committed to outworking everybody while I acquired the knowledge and skills needed to succeed.

From that point forward, month after month, I racked up record sales and was on my way to a long and rewarding career #2... the highlights and most memorable lessons of which I'll pass onto you in the following pages.

Career #2 (40 years of double-digit growth)

1980 – 1990: Copyline, sold to IKON Office Solutions

- Revenue increase: Growth rate of 15% annually
- Entry level sales then general sales manager

1991 – 2005: MWB Business Systems, acquired by Imagine Technology Group then Global Imaging, and finally by Xerox

- Revenue increase: Growth rate of 29% annually
- MWB partner and VP of sales, then president, and CEO

2005 – 2007: ConfirmNet, was later sold to Ebix

- Revenue increase: Growth Rate of 600%
- CEO/president

2007 – present: Rollins Consulting Group

- Coached several hundred CEOs of companies with revenues from $1 million to $3 billion

2008 to 2011: Imaging Plus, Inc.

- Revenue Increase: Growth rate of 66% annually

- Partner

2011 – 2019: Solis Capital Partners

- Advisor to operating partners

2012 – present: Sage Executive Group

- 130 members and growing, with companies from $1 million to $3 billion in revenue
- Co-founder and CEO

Advisory Boards: Bird Rock Systems, Solis Capital Partners, F & F Income Properties, LLC

CHAPTER 2
The Game Plan

It takes just as much energy to wish as it does to plan.
—*Eleanor Roosevelt*

Wish in one hand, spit in the other and see which gets full first.
—*Betty Jean Jones (My Mother In Law)*

WHAT'S THE PLAN?

WINNING TEAMS PLAN

There are many parallels between winning sports teams and successful companies. Even at the NHL level, some teams I joined were unquestionably better than others, and in the corporate world, too, I encountered both great and not-so-great companies. I was well into my second career when I discovered one definitive commonality amongst those stand-out hockey teams and companies: They all had simple game plans with clearly defined goals that everyone knew and understood. The others had no plan and therefore, unrealistic expectations of their personnel.

Despite amazing talent, a sports team or business without a playbook will fail. Even a bad plan well-performed and focused on daily will defeat no plan at all most of the time. For example, if you're driving to Miami from Nashville without a GPS or any directions and simply hoping that you'll eventually arrive, you'd get there faster riding a bike with just a map.

It may be hard to believe, but none of the eight pro teams I played on had clearly defined strategies for team members. In pro sports, the assumption was that everyone knew what to do, (and we did when it came to our individual jobs). However, having never played together before, no one understood their goals as part of a cohesive unit.

The same could be said of business team members with undefined company-wide goals. Goals must be specific to each person's role and distinctly aligned with the organizational plan so employees can see how their individual performances affect the whole team. When leaders in sports or business leave it up to their people to figure things out, the result becomes an "everyone for themselves" mentality instead of a team-focused one.

Goals must be comprehensive, detailed, tangible and accessible— not simply the fluctuating hopes and dreams of out-of-touch, frenetic company owners. Many businesses experience chaos because the leaders think that team members know what's expected of them. In reality, they haven't a clue about the company's direction or any plan to get there. People can't be expected to support a business and/or vision if they don't even know where it's headed. No surprise then that those same companies often fall short of achieving their unseen, unshared goals.

The few times there were game plans where I worked, I was good at getting teams to implement them. I had a precise vision of what success would look like and stuck to it, modified it when circumstances changed, and ultimately achieved it. However, always in the back of my mind I felt that the game plans were flawed in some ways and I knew I wanted to create my own one day.

Unconsciously, I began collecting and storing away information for my business plans before I even thought about writing it down or developing it further on my own. It wasn't until I felt confident that I'd read, witnessed, and heard it all when it came to business plans (and the fallout from a lack thereof), that I devised my own.

FAIL TO PLAN, PLAN TO FAIL

Whether you're at the startup stage or have been in business for years, a plan sets the tone for an organization and helps focus its brand. Businesses fail or succeed depending upon its leadership's planning. Plans take the visions of owners (and coaches, in sports) and put them into words on paper, so anyone can act on them at any time.

Plans:

- clarify business goals.
- spell out the necessary leadership, duties and skills of all employees.
- outline how to proceed in any given situation.
- map out the most efficient pathways to achieve success.

Having a plan is less about forecasting the future, and more about setting attainable goals and making changes as the company evolves.

Companies without plans (or those with unused ones):

- aren't firing on all cylinders because without specific budgets, goals and planned strategies, people will aimlessly struggle to produce results. Daily actions will most likely be indiscriminate and reactive compared to those businesses executing a well-thought-out business plan.
- don't know who they are as businesses and run the risk of missing sales projections because they haven't researched their market segments. Before opening a business, companies can avoid this major mistake by researching and outlining specifics, such as where to sell and how many employees will be needed.
- could run out of cash before the doors open because owners didn't anticipate startup costs.

- can't hold team members accountable if they don't have any definable goals or know what they are. Trying to hold people accountable to targets and goals that aren't relevant, realistic, or properly defined or communicated is guaranteed failure.

I see companies that actually think about writing business plans for the new year but come January 1 they're still MIA. That's when I'll get a bunch of SOS (sh#t, oh, sh#t!) calls from CEOs needing help on plans that should have been done months before.

So, what happens to those companies that chronically don't think about planning until after the year has begun? If the economy's good, luck will keep them alive and they may survive short-term, but they'll never thrive. Those one-hit wonders in sports or business can only sustain themselves for about three years. Sometimes owners with good timing sell their companies for a ton of money and all of a sudden everyone thinks that they're experts… until they fail miserably going forward because it was luck and had nothing to do with ability. You need a plan to progress.

THE EMPEROR'S NEW PLAN

I've worked with hundreds of CEOs and inconceivably about 90% of the smaller $1 million to $5 million companies had no current written plans. Among the larger, $5 million plus businesses, roughly 70% operated without them. The unoriginal excuses from leaders ring in my ear on a loop:

Excuse #1: We have one, but don't really use it.

Excuse #2: I think we have one. I'm just not sure where.

Excuse #3: We have one, but it's outdated.

Excuse #4: We're going to do one, but we haven't had the time.

Excuse #5: We have one, although it's not written down. The owner knows it.

In essence, these companies have no plans. If team members can't see it, don't know it, can't understand it, aren't living it, and aren't committed to it, then there isn't one. It's like the infamous question, *"Do you work out?"* Everyone says they do but probing further you discover many haven't worked out in some time for one reason or another. (FYI: According to the Statistic Brain Research Institute, 67% of people with gym memberships never use them—but, no doubt, like our plan-less leaders intend to one day.)

THE CEO HURDLE

Show me a dysfunctional company or team and I'll show you bad leadership. Senior leadership teams often focus only on the bigger picture and the company's long-term strategies, however, this approach is usually disconnected from the day-to-day operations. We've all known one of those bosses. Flawed leaders who think that their ways are the only ways and who don't bother getting input from their teams. Ego is the fastest way to kill a business.

Leaders must be one-hundred percent committed to the same values and practices that they demand of their employees. Improving performance starts at the top, and when it comes to planning, leaders need to recognize whether they're part of the solution or problem.

According to the experts, the biggest challenges or obstacles companies face in achieving their annual goals and budgets are the CEOs or owners. Here are the most common reasons why:

1. They think they're smarter than everyone so no one else can contribute.

2. They're afraid to commit because plans require follow-up and then leaders have to be accountable, too. If they say they're going to do something then they've actually got to do it.

3. New business owners can get carried away, believing their passion is enough to build a thriving company.

4. Planning takes effort, and it's easier to just continue the status quo instead of reinventing themselves and striving to improve.

5. Sometimes owners of already-successful businesses, and particularly those with substantially increasing revenues, would rather avoid answering to company executives who'd want to know about their commensurate raises or compensation.

6. Some leaders just don't know how to plan because they never had training and would prefer to avoid people talking about, or judging, what they're doing.

Whenever the feedback confirms that the CEO, CFO or person leading the company is the issue, changes must be made. CEOs have to be willing to listen and assume responsibility for their own shortcomings, then adjust. One way to find out whether or not a leader is an impediment to progress is by conducting anonymous 360° reviews from coworkers. Self-actualized leaders want honest, objective feedback from people inside and outside of the company. Leaders who reject that notion raise big red flags.

Sometimes the problem may be that employees and managers tend to keep CEOs insulated, so bosses are often the last to know things. Leaders must provide a safe environment where employees feel comfortable to confide in them or reach out to senior management for help—and must make it clear that no one is above the law, no matter the title or clout.

I think about the newsmen, for instance, who have recently made headlines regarding sexual harassment in the workplace. It's been going on for many years but once it became public and the very profitable news programs began to be affected, the shareholders and boards of directors knew it too and couldn't look the other way. Now, if there's a whiff of impropriety, heads roll right out the door. Anonymous surveys would have revealed to network honchos what had been going on.

BEGIN HERE

A business plan needs to start with everyone's input from the ground up, not from the top down. Unfortunately, it's usually the opposite in big companies. Most corporations do all the planning at the executive level without feedback from the frontline employees—which is why team members often don't know what to do, when to do it by, or how their jobs affect the company's bottom line.

Team budgets and targets come from the master plan and individual goals are discussed and determined between department heads and teams. Sales team members are assigned goals relevant to revenue, operations team members receive cost-related goals, and so on. If a company does $10 million in revenue, for example, its plan may direct that $3 million come from one department, $3 million from another and $4 million from another, and that everyone within those departments have responsibilities for either revenue or expenses. The most important part of those financials though, is that a person or a group of people fills every line item or task and is accountable for its contents. For example, if it's a telephone expense then somebody owns that, making more or less money based on how he or she manages that.

It's the leader's duty to translate organizational goals, budgets and incentives into clearly defined, attainable and measurable individual targets with short-term and long-term deadlines, so employees can evaluate their progress. When goals are vague and ambiguous, the results will be disappointing.

After leaders deliver a plan to their teams, I suggest they ask every team member two questions:

1. **What is his or her specific role in the plan?** All employees must confirm they know exactly what's expected of them.

2. **What's in it for him or her?** All team members must have   a clear understanding of what success looks like, and their stake in it.

> **Companies that plan grow 30% faster
> than those that don't[1].**

Same Story, Different Company

I'm pleased to say there was an actual plan at the first company I worked for as an entry-level salesperson. We stuck to the simple plan, winning more times than we lost, and grew the business successfully. After the company sold, I passed on going into leadership with the new public firm and decided instead to see what life was like at a bigger organization. I took a job as one of twenty-four regional managers for a multibillion-dollar, worldwide company that makes electronic products.

Before I arrived, my position had constant turnover and was the worst-performing territory in the country. With absolutely no support, I applied my plan—consisting of the dos and don'ts I'd picked up so far—and my region climbed to number two within eleven months. Shortly after, leadership offered me a

---

1   Source: Journal of Management Studies

promotion to national sales manager, but it became evident that with the giant company came all of the responsibility and no authority. It was time to claim a leadership role and take more control of my destiny, which I figured a small private company would provide. I left my position and quickly secured a role—with equity for the first time—at a family business focused on document imaging and office equipment with $3.2 million in retail revenue.

My new company had a plan, but it was hidden in a drawer. This factor contributed to their lack of growth in their direct business. Technically there was a plan, but management didn't utilize it and the employees didn't know it existed. A year before, they had paid $5,000 for this business plan, sitting in a binder about 3 1/2 inches thick and written by an MBA. No doubt, the MBA spent countless hours interviewing the CEO and documenting his projections as it was really a wish list of unrealistic goals. Then, those pie-in-the-sky expectations were directed to the owners and management team, who funneled the intangible directives to the rest of the employees. I discovered the unused plan in a dusty cabinet drawer in a corner of the CEO's office and about 99% of it was crap.

So, the first thing I did was interview the leaders of the top five established, $20-million companies located in the same market area in Southern California. I wanted to determine why they all held steady at $20 million in revenue, yet never grew. At $20 million in revenue, these *lifestyle* business owners all agreed they made enough money to live comfortably and had no desire to risk expansion and jeopardize the status quo. Also, being the major drivers of the business, they tended to depend on one or a few key people, and didn't spend the time, energy and money developing their teams or individuals. What this told me was that owners who did plan for growth and employee improvement could attain much greater income and success.

Next, I converted the plan to a half dozen sheets of paper, copied it—and in those days—transferred it onto transparencies. After I crossed out the last year it'd been used and penciled in the current one, I projected our new business plan onto the wall. Each box, or job, was assigned to someone and everyone knew exactly what they were responsible for. I offered all the support and resources anyone needed to do their jobs, but if employees still couldn't perform then they understood that a) they wouldn't make the kind of money they wanted, or b) there would soon be other people in their seats.

I applied the concepts I'd collected so far from other teams' playbooks—recruiting great players, training and coaching them daily, and making them accountable. I created an environment that was competitive but fair, making sure my people knew I always had their backs. The next three years the company revenue was $5.4 million, $7 million, and $12 million respectively, and we made it happen without major cash infusions—instead bootstrapping and building great teams with almost no employee turnover. Within eight years, the company was at $30 million in annual revenue.

As I rose through the ranks from Partner and VP of Sales to President and CEO, I continued to fine-tune and execute my plan throughout multiple acquisitions of the company. With each sale or acquisition, it was like the Bill Murray movie *Groundhog Day*—the same thing all over again. The business plan either sat unused in a drawer or was regarded like folklore—some elusive concept floating around in the CEO's head rather than in a living, breathing document.

The next company I joined as CEO/President had been stalled for seven years. Although they had a good idea, it'd been going nowhere for many years, experiencing constant turnover in leadership—five managers in four years. Investors kept hiring the talking heads and plugging them in without direction or distinct goals. Then, without assistance or motivation to improve, the managers got frustrated and left. It's hard to imagine multibillion-dollar, international corporations would crash and burn this way. We implemented a plan to grow, started focusing on the correct customers, reconfigured the team and grew the revenues fourfold in the 18 months I was running the company.

Jumping on the Plan Wagon

One company I worked with early in my business-coaching career, had achieved $80 million in revenue without an official plan—only budgets and the amazing visions of the owners. The rest of the team had to blindly zigzag with leaders as they went. Finally, after almost 15 years in business, leadership formally developed a plan with the entire team's input. With that came alignment, consistency between all objectives, and processes that supported long-term goals. Since implementing a written plan, the company has far outpaced any other in the industry, with around a quarter of a billion dollars annual revenue and over 1,100 employees.

Plans Change, So Change Plans

VISION WITH RESTRAINT

A plan and a vision are two different things. For example, an owner and general manager of a new NHL franchise may have a vision to win the Stanley cup in three years, but their goal is to not embarrass themselves the first year and win more games than they lose. Leaders need visions to achieve greater things in the future, but having a business plan that everyone believes in is vital for today.

While visions can be grandiose, plans (like goals) should be precise, methodical steps that are reviewed and adjusted quarterly and annually. The days of ten-year planning are behind us. Even a five-year business plan that includes budgets, strategy and head count will become irrelevant with how quickly market conditions and technology change. For example, just five years ago Nordstrom's strategy revolved around stores, stores, stores! Today, the high-end global retailer focuses on mobile and online sales with stores in strategic locations. Leadership saw how the marketplace was changing and modified its plan by amping up millennial-focused agendas. Good planning takes all present and future possibilities into account.

In sports, too, management and coaches must plan for change. If a starting goalie gets hurt, for example, the game plan has to accommodate the back-up goalie's strengths. So, having a vision of where you want to be in a few years, and planning for cash and banking needs eighteen to twenty-four months ahead based on growth are valid, as long as you remain flexible enough to adjust plans as you go. Think long-term but act short-term.

BANKING ON NO CHANGE

In the early 1990s, during the bank consolidation era, one of the smaller ($10 million in revenue) companies I worked for was represented by a worldwide banking giant instead of a more suitable community bank where we'd be on a first-name basis with the president. So, when Bank of America bought Security Pacific and we didn't fit the new profile—with no banking or credit facility back-up—our company almost tanked.

Leadership scrambled to come up with a revised business plan for survival, and within 48 hours laid off 30% of the workforce (with severance) and issued pay cuts for the remaining employees. We focused on cash management and generation, cutting all unnecessary expenditures, and net income instead of revenue—parting ways with customers who weren't profitable. Next, we shared our story and action plan with a community bank that we engaged within 60 days.

Eventually, good came out of this process since we discovered that the business had been overstaffed and could run with fewer people. As a result, we rehired only the A players and never ran *fat* again. Best of all, we learned that we were survivors able to ride out the storm...

...until a few years later when we found ourselves in a similar situation. A mortgage company representing a significant percentage of our revenue was acquired by a top 5 banking giant. At the same time, another large national bank that was our client declared bankruptcy. These two factors caused a devastating drop in revenue within a short period of time. Any time one or two clients represents a significant part of a company's revenue, that's a problem called *business concentration*. For example, if a business has 100 clients and one client represents $5 million of its $10 million revenue that's taking a costly chance. After that, instead of recruiting $1-million to $8-million clients, we sought out twenty $500,000 clients.

The 2008 banking crisis—the worst economic disaster since the Great Depression of 1929—also notoriously illustrated what happens when companies don't anticipate change. All of the banks pulled their lines of credit within a 30-day period, and financial institutions which issued, bought (often with borrowed money) or insured loans didn't plan on countless people defaulting on theirs. It ruined thousands of businesses that didn't see it coming. I was a chairman of a $100 million company at the time that had 100% of its revenue concentrated in one area. The company plunged to $60 million overnight, forcing us to let go of many employees.

If owners don't plan for and face the future, their companies can become statistics.

Bad News Travels Fast

In 2009, President Obama didn't grasp the weight his words carried. A misinterpreted five-second sound byte about government bailouts and big companies no longer sending employees to Vegas, left countless people believing that the 44th U.S. President didn't want them to go to Sin City. What he meant was *not on the taxpayer's dime.*

As a result, tens of thousands of Las Vegas hotel rooms booked for conferences were canceled within the month and the city suffered a significant decline in revenue from both conventions and visitors for years after. Though he didn't do it purposely, the President almost crippled an industry, which wasn't prepared for such a catastrophic downturn of events.

Two Plans are Better than One

For tomorrow belongs to the people
who prepare for it today.
– African proverb

SWOT FIRST

Before every hockey game, our team did an analysis of all opponents to help us figure out how to win against them and the way that each team member could contribute and increase the odds. In the equally-competitive business world, analyzing your own company first is also critical to success. A SWOT analysis is a business tool that offers invaluable information and examines not only the company and employees, but also the industry, competitors, economy and more.

SWOT is an acronym for *strengths, weaknesses, opportunities* and *threats*. Strengths and weaknesses are internal to a company, coming from within an organization and can be controlled. Opportunities and threats are external to a company and can't be controlled, but they can be planned for. SWOTs are immensely useful to owners and I recommend conducting one annually at minimum.

AN ANALYSIS OF THE ACRONYM

Asking the right questions of all of your team members will provide answers about a company's strengths, weaknesses, opportunities and threats.

Strengths:

- *What does the company do better than competitors?*
- *What areas of the business are most profitable?*
- *Why do you choose to work at this company?*

Strengths are your key differentiators, those things that set one business apart from its competitors—a culture, a product or the customers it serves are just some examples. Sage Executive Group's strength, for instance, is its coaches—accomplished business leaders we select carefully before granting membership. Another strength is Sage's lack of turnover; when people join, they get a lot of value and stay.

Weaknesses:

- Does the company lack a business plan? What about a management training program? An equity plan, or financing?

- Is the company's bank limiting the company's growth?

- Are long-term key managers tied into the success of the business, or can they leave for another company at any time?

- What internal resources are lacking?

- What areas of the business aren't very profitable?

- Where does the company need further education and/ or experience?

Weaknesses are areas (such as excessive turnover, high debt or inadequate capital) which prevent companies from performing at their optimum levels and remaining competitive.

Opportunities:

- *How can the business do more for its customers?*

- *Are there related products and/or services that provide an opportunity for growth?*

- *Can technology further enhance the business?*

Opportunities could be increasing the sales team, finding a bank that finances growth or bringing additional investment into the business. In other words, *what are the things the company could do but hasn't?*

Threats:

- *What obstacles does the business face?*

- What are competitors doing that your company isn't?

- *What's happening in the economy and industry?*

- *Is the company an industry leader or is it just bumping along the road like most others?*

A pandemic such as COVID-19, a banking crisis, a stock market crash or the latest technology (which many businesses fear will replace the need for countless products and services) are examples of external threats. The companies that just follow trends will eventually go away, so the others need to prepare and keep an eye out for what the future may bring.

WHY NOT SWOT?

A plan written without a SWOT is virtually worthless because without input from teams, it won't be relevant. A SWOT reveals what companies are doing well, where improvement is needed and what should be eliminated according to a consensus. You'd be amazed at how many stupid processes are discovered this way.

When I do a SWOT with companies I have every team member fill it out independently, in a confidential manner, so everyone can comment freely. I find that's beneficial in both private and public companies because once you're in a room with a CEO there's often only one opinion. This analysis is where the elephant in the room—the thing that everybody knows but is too afraid to approach the CEO about—gets called out. A strong leader though, appreciates getting impartial input from other VPs and managers before sharing results with the planning committee.

A SWOT helps consolidate commonalities. An observation from one of fifteen people is just a feeling, but twelve of fifteen in agreement about what's not working is an issue that needs addressing. Without that consensus, those issues are rarely solved, especially if a CEO doesn't agree. Even if things are great, doing a SWOT is an opportunity to evaluate issues that may have been overlooked. It's also a good team exercise to keep tabs on company alignment. Keep in mind, however, any analysis is only as good as the information that produces it. If the organizations find it difficult to be honest then the results may be skewed. (A sample SWOT analysis can be found in the Resource section.)

BUSINESS PLAN BASICS

I think every business owner should plan in two areas— professionally and personally—and both are of equal importance. Plans don't have to be complicated, just complete.

The fundamental elements of a business plan include:

Values: The principles that affect the way a company conducts business and interacts with customers, partners, shareholders and employees. Values must be genuine, not just pithy taglines on paper.

A CEO has to be the primary example of a company's values by living them and making them real. The best CEO I ever worked for was Mike Moffett, a great role model and leader, who knew that values lead to results. He sent letters to all new customers promising if they were unhappy with any aspect of his company's services or products he'd address it personally and included his contact information. He built a company around those customer service values and his employees knew they'd have to deliver, or the boss would hear about it. In my opinion, any company leader unwilling to take a call from a dissatisfied customer's call should be fired.

Vision: The hopes and dreams for a business and the framework for planning, a vision describes what company founders are trying to build and answers the question, *where is the company headed in the next 5 years and exactly where will we be then?*

Mission: A company's purpose for those in the organization and its customers, the mission answers the question, *why does the company exist? (Note*: Employees who can't grasp the company's purpose typically lack inspiration and passion. They may achieve short-term results, but they won't have what it takes for the long haul.)

Key Metrics: Measurable goals for the company and each team member.

Budgets: The business scorecards that are reviewed regularly without fail.

Good Value

Core values are an essential and guiding force for a growing company, and there isn't just one correct way to conceive them. A company I know, which provides online marketing services, utilizes the acronym *DATA* to define its company's values.

Dedicated Fans – valued employees

Accountability – to customers and fellow employees

Team – exceptional by hiring, firing and training aggressively

Adaptability – strive for progress, take risks, re-evaluate constantly, learn and adapt

Some Plans are Personal

> When someone gets between you and your goals, the best thing to do is pull his shirt over his head and punch him in the face a few times.

Whether someone wants to take on new challenges, enhance his or her work performance or change unhealthy habits—creating a personal development plan is the best way to ensure success.

Personal development is as unique as the individual plotting it, but everyone should make it a priority. While some people methodically reach their aspirations, there are others who lose direction and consistently struggle. What differentiates these two groups? Having inspiration and a plan. A solid, detailed map helps direct all actions toward goals, and instills more confidence and prevents deviation.

Personal plans are written just like business plans and are good for everybody at every level. When working with employees one-on- one (which I suggest all group leaders do) I first ask them to do appraisals of who they are now and who they want to be. Then, I advise them that if they don't like the answers, they can devise a plan to change things. This is the part where people tend to make excuses, blaming their childhoods, poor education, challenges or other difficulties for their lack of forward momentum or improvement.

Next, I encourage employees to set goals in categories that are important to them:

Family: Have family members help define this category. Maybe it's important to divide the parental duties of two working parents. If a goal is to have at least one parent at every afternoon soccer game, for example, both parents' jobs must be flexible enough to accommodate this without their respective companies suffering from their absences.

Finances/Budgets: People who keep score of their net worth and measure it annually grow this category.

Credit: Keep this category to a minimum, but if it's already in dire straits, then devise a step-by-step plan to take care of it. My in-laws taught me that if you can't buy something for cash, you really can't afford it.

Savings: I've known many couples who decided to diligently save one salary. I have close family members who always banked one of their paychecks and the payoff was retiring early. It wasn't easy and took discipline, but they now live a very comfortable life. It's the exception but should be the rule.

If that's not manageable, then people should at least have a plan to put away 10% of every paycheck. Just like giving or tithing, 10% has been the long-standing suggested contribution to a religious organization and it's also a good amount to save or pay yourself right off the top. It beats counting on social security benefits and/or waiting for elderly parents to die, which sadly are the only plans many adults have these days.

Health: Keep an up-to-date health scorecard that includes annual checkup results, weight targets, blood pressure, cholesterol, nutrition goals, etc. We can only do our best to mitigate health challenges by making smart choices especially when it comes to what we put into our bodies. As the Yiddish proverb goes, *Man plans, God Laughs.* Even planning can't help if you're dealt a bad hand in the health category.

Fitness: Keep track of goals and acknowledge progress. I use my Fitbit to set fitness goals and measure my daily steps, calorie intake, etc. I also stick to a Paleo diet with weekends off, only giving into my ice-cream habit when I reach 15,000 daily steps (which is every day!).

Mindfulness: Daily meditation and continued learning can help improve all aspects of life.

Planning Like There's No Tomorrow

- As seventy-six million baby boomers approach retirement, well over half don't have enough money to last through their old age and 44% don't have wills which is bad news for their millennial offspring.*

- Seniors who rely on Social Security for half their income: 61%.**

- Among elderly Social Security beneficiaries, 21% of married couples and about 43% of unmarried persons rely on Social Security for 90% or more of their income.**

- Among women aged eighty and older, Social Security provides the majority of income for 72% of beneficiaries.**

*(Source: The National Institute of Retirement Security)
**(Source: Social Security Administration)

Who Cares?

People don't care how much you know, until they know how much you care. -John C. Maxwell

The benefits of planning in general are well-known and widespread. According to the experts, people who plan are less tense because planning is an efficient stress management technique. When people prepare rather than let things just happen, they minimize or even prevent feeling anxious. What's more, happier people are more productive employees, and more productive employees lead to happy customers and owners.

Most people who struggle just need a hand or some direction to make positive changes. The CEOs like the ones I coach genuinely care and encourage their people to plan both professionally and personally, and in return gain enduring, hard-working, loyal employees. Conversely, when employees have personal difficulties or constant financial and personal turmoil it often leads to them missing work, showing up late, leaving early, and even substance abuse. Winning leaders, like winning sports coaches, know they not only depend on, but can also profoundly impact, how their team members perform. Those leaders step up and take a sincere, comprehensive interest in their employees' lives. If they don't, society will undoubtedly bear the burden.

Many great companies bring in a variety of coaches and advisors for their team members and the payoff is huge. For example, companies could show they care by hosting a *Lunch & Learn*, where owners provide food and invite a financial advisor to talk with their teams about planning for the future. The following month, perhaps a nutritionist or a fitness expert could speak. These days, with runaway healthcare costs, if business owners pay more attention to the full wellbeing of their employees they'll realize a direct cost benefit—and if they don't, they'll just pay more. The proof is in the research:

- A majority 67% of employers identified employees' poor health habits as one of their top three challenges to maintaining affordable health coverage. (Source: U.S. Centers for Disease Control and Prevention)

- Employees who are healthy eaters are 25% more likely to have higher job performance, and those who exercise for at least thirty minutes, three times a week, perform 15% better. In addition, absenteeism is 27% lower for workers who eat healthy and exercise regularly. (Source: Health Enhancement Research Organization)

- Overweight employees cost their employers $73.1 billion annually and file twice the number of workers' compensation claims. (Source: U.S. Department of Health and Human Services)

CHAPTER 3
Building Great Teams: In it to Win it

Teams Built to Last: What it Takes

TO BE OR NOT TO BE ENGAGED

Great teams generate great results, but these teams don't just happen by chance. Building successful teams starts with hiring the right people, with the right combination of professional abilities, and then molding and coaching them into winning teams. That's why great leaders create great teams. Leaders who stress the value of teamwork, and effectively teach their team members to collaborate on common goals, maximize their successes. Lone wolves (even if they're excellent producers) aren't as valuable to businesses as those who can achieve results with others collectively.

In pro sports, if athletes can't perform there are others waiting in the wings being groomed to replace them. Throughout our hockey careers, my dad and I felt the looming pressure of younger, cheaper, faster and stronger players. That feeling—that fear—followed me into the business world. I worked extra hard knowing there were always people who had more education or a higher proficiency with technology, a willingness to work longer hours for less pay and an eagerness to take my place. Although all employees should feel that same urgency, current statistics prove that's rarely the case.

STATUS: NOT ENGAGED

According to Gallup's State of the American Workplace Report (2016), there are three categories of U.S. employee engagement:

Engaged Employees	33%
Disengaged Employees	50%
Actively Disengaged Employees	17%

This means only 33% of people are committed to, and enthusiastic about, their jobs and/or in jobs that align with their specific strengths. The remaining 67% and majority of the average workforce, is disengaged to various degrees. (If I applied these numbers to the professional sports teams my father and I played on these percentages would also hold true.)

The 50% of disengaged employees show up and throw up, contributing only what's expected of them. Most companies don't have hiring strategies based on company goals, yet they wonder why team members are disengaged. Without a plan for successful hiring, managers are likely to acquire the wrong people, then have trouble managing them.

The 17% of actively disengaged employees are emotionally disconnected from their companies and may actually be working against their employers' interests. They're unproductive and more likely to negatively influence their coworkers, miss workdays, show up late, cheat on time cards and expense reports, steal from their companies and drive customers away. Gallup estimates that actively disengaged employees cost the U.S. $450 billion to $550 billion in lost productivity per year.

Categories of engaged, disengaged and actively disengaged can be broken down further into sub-categories. Of the 50% who are disengaged, the top 20% are the people trying to get better, the middle 10% don't care, and the bottom 20% care even less and may end up actively disengaged. The actively disengaged employees certainly don't move anything forward, represent a negative disruptive force within any business and are on their way out. Even among the top 33% not everyone's created equal. For example, if you ask a leadership team of ten, "Who's the best on the team?" You'll find that it's always one or two people that everyone looks up to.

I attribute the lack of employee engagement to the following three factors:

1. The absence of a game plan that everyone on the team understands and owns.

2. A lack of manager-employee communication.

3. Leadership's lack of commitment to continuous improvement by keeping employees around who don't make the grade.

Strictly Business

The former General Electric Company chairman and CEO Jack Welch (who recently passed away) staunchly believed that the bottom 10% of employees should be let go. I used to think that was severe, but now think it's soft. When you're making money and things are going well, then everybody's a genius so leaving things (and the bottom 10% performers) alone is easy. Of course, as soon as the economy turns a quarter-inch everyone panics and reacts instead of already being prepared.

Welch was highly criticized for his 10% rule, but since he left GE has struggled. Recently the company announced it can't continue to grow and will divest a significant portion to get earnings back on track. GE also dropped off the Dow Jones Industrial Average (DJIA) index after a century there.

MANAGERS MAKE THE TEAM

Team leaders can hope team members adjust and work well together eventually, or they can ensure success by setting some guidelines that consider and capitalize on the uniqueness each employee brings to the table.

Managers contribute to great teams by:

- spelling out what's expected of all team members and providing clear performance standards and deadlines.

- regularly checking team members' progress and staying on top of issues before they escalate.

- encouraging employees to adopt company values by modeling them.

- prompting team members to contribute and share information, and remain open to each other's ideas, suggestions and concerns.

- consistently steering members toward the team's overall goals.

- being accessible to offer help and backup.

- valuing the roles of all team members.

- acknowledging and rewarding teamwork.

BUILDING SUPPORT

If managers want productive teams they must do everything to ensure team members gel. That's not always an easy feat considering that each person claims a unique set of strengths and weaknesses. Team-building activities can be both fun and beneficial and enhance skills such as planning, problem-solving and conflict resolution. They also give management and employees opportunities to see each other in a different light, thereby, increasing trust and morale. These constructive games prompt communication and deeper discussion, which lead to real connections—these are all important components of strong teams.

I use several team-building exercises that help teammates engage in getting to know and understand each other better. One is the classic *Two Truths and a Lie*. Each person tells two true statements and one lie about themselves and their colleagues have to guess which is bogus. I also use *Around the World* for both members of company teams and peer groups as a way to find out about everyone's early years and break the ice. Each participant takes steps around the room and visits up to 10 stops (taking one step per stop). Each stop signifies a significant moment in life, from when someone was born to the present day. Sometimes it is good to use pictures or objects to illustrate life events.

COMPLACENCY: A COMPANY KILLER

Great leaders of sports dynasties and long-running businesses recognize that improvement is unending. It's constantly examining and tweaking their rosters during both good and bad times. Companies without deep benches (or development systems that consistently educate and motivate employees to grow), become hostages of their own incompetence, and get stuck with inadequate and ineffective employees just taking up space.

Complacency is a pervasive disease that impedes progress, innovation and success, both personally and professionally. The bottom half of the disengaged and all of the actively disengaged employees usually remain in the company because management gets lazy, or complacent, and doesn't keep up with measuring progress or recognizing the score. After all, it takes a good deal of time and effort to replace someone. Other leading excuses why managers keep disengaged staff around include:

- the numbers are okay and the company made some money last year, so they think, *Why hire someone else?*

- they mistakenly believe that they can't find a replacement for an under-performing employee because the job has never been done by anyone else. (*Translation:* There's no official process in place for finding new people.)

- they're getting by and a new hire will likely be no better, which is probably true based on poor hiring practices.

- they fear repercussions from higher up.

- they can't fire many non-performers because they've been around forever.

Managers are responsible for working with those team members that fall short, doing a better job of reviewing efforts and finding solutions and incentives to make all employees feel attached to the outcome. When every employee—from the back door to the top floor—is committed to their goals, great things happen.

In the warehouse of a company where I was the CEO, we had an amazing leader who kept his performance-driven team responsible for, and motivated by, daily goals relating to the inventory, line item amounts and shipments. Although we processed tens of millions of dollars of products each year, our inventory variances remained negligible. This was because whenever a big increase in product and dollars were projected, the warehouse employees had autonomy to decide how that would be accomplished. For example, they could choose whether to hire more people or share those would-be salaries and... wait for it... *work harder.* They usually opted for the money or a combination of hiring minimal new employees and dividing the unused wages proportionately based on performance.

COMPLACENCY COSTS

In the 1980s, when experts believed that the Japanese economy was on the verge of global domination, a guarantee of permanent employment was looked upon favorably—but not anymore. In reality it meant that an employee didn't have to be good for life, he or she just had to show up to receive increases for each year of service. Production ultimately plummeted, and companies were forced to cut costs by hiring temporary workers, who were paid lower wages, weren't entitled to most benefits or job security and therefore, had little incentive to work. Employees who left to work for other businesses, started again on the low end of the new company's pay scale. Now, temporary and unmotivated employees make up one-third of Japan's workforce.

Who's on Your Team...and Why?

SACRED COWS, SLUGS, AND MORE

If a business isn't weeding out problem employees, then it's contributing to a leakage of quality people and compromising the company culture. Firing employees isn't fun, but strong managers should be ready and brave enough to go head-to-head with the big boss when they feel it's necessary for the sake of their teams. Especially when it comes to the employees that corrupt company culture. Do you recognize any of the culprits below on your teams?

THE SACRED COWS:

They represent a group of unqualified employees rarely discussed in companies but found everywhere. SCs can be anyone from an investor's relative, to the best friend of one of the owners. I've seen it all, including a CEO's former secretary promoted to VP of HR with no training, knowledge or ability to manage in that position. SCs are unmotivated and difficult to fire for obvious reasons.

THE SLUGS:

These virtual benchwarmers are content doing what they're doing, making what they're making and don't want anything to change. They're both young and old, long-term and new employees who go through the motions, feeling no attachment to their jobs. Slugs include the actively disengaged and are part of this endemic issue affecting team performance.

THE MISGUIDED:

They're usually employees who were hired for jobs, or transferred into ones, that weren't right for them.

In sports, for example, it'd be unreasonable to expect that a physical defenseman like me could score goals as well as a skilled forward. In business, maybe employees who were originally good at their jobs were moved to positions they weren't trained for, or outgrew their skill level. These are mostly smart, hard-working employees but when evaluated, they're just not performing. If these people are put in the right roles though, they often shine.

THE UNTOUCHABLES (I REFER TO THEM AS ON BOARD TERRORISTS):

These long-term employees virtually hold companies hostage by not being accountable to anyone. Based on their impressive numbers, these self-centered, top producers who lack any concept of team tend to get away with bad behavior. I've encountered countless untouchables, and the times when I exhibited the character and courage to hold them accountable were always defining moments. Whenever the powers that be did intervene, not willing to risk letting the person go, I knew it was time for me to move on. Still, whenever I succeeded in getting rid of an untouchable to survive another day—a feat my coworkers thought impossible—the improvements in culture and company performance were staggering.

A Matter of Principle

The Pareto principle, better known as the 80/20 rule, states that about 80% of the effects come from 20% of the causes. Applied to business, roughly 20% of the employees are producing 80% of the revenue. Not having a pool of people to choose from, managers hang onto the 80% and like parents of the proverbial problem children, wind up spending most of their time on them. It's only when companies employ the right hiring and training practices that they'll always have someone ready to step up at every level.

GREAT PLAYERS, GREAT TEAMS

Effective teams require people with different strengths working together to achieve the best results. Teamwork is everyone's responsibility, but managers must choose the best team players.

All great team players:

- are prepared to play.
- always expect to win.
- have a plan that they're committed to.
- continually train, learn, improve and practice their crafts.
- show persistence in the face of adversity.
- share the same vision and values for the company's success.

- accept accountability for their performance.
- celebrate the wins and payoffs of working hard.

ALL THE DIFFERENCE

On commitment: *99% is a bitch, 100% is a breeze* -Jack Canfield

To me, that 1% is the difference between being good and great. Going above and beyond seems to be a lost art these days, so those who do should be rewarded and promoted. In business or sports, I'd rather be in the bottom fraction of the 1% (the worst of the best) than the top percentage of the 99%. That's a huge separation in terms of earnings and opportunities.

It's All About the Culture

CREATE A CULTURE

Company culture is a business' identity, and refers to the work environment and company's values, along with the attitudes and behaviors that direct and influence management's interaction with team members. There's no denying that the culture affects every aspect of a company and can make or break a business. Research shows that the highest-rated companies also have the highest-rated cultures and the opposite is also true. Creating company culture is a crucial executive responsibility. Managers should be expected to help further an atmosphere that people want to be part of, and that makes them feel their contributions are valued. Those people, in return, will often surpass expectations rather than leave the company or become part of the disengaged group.

Everything leadership says about the culture must be true, because if you get good people and put them in a contaminated culture, they're not going to last long. When building a great culture, leaders need to know about their team members, who they are, what they do and what drives them. Investing time and money in people who truly specialize in the roles businesses need will have immense payoffs later for both companies and employees. Alternately, hiring people just to have warm bodies fill chairs is counter-productive for not only teams, but entire companies. It's just a matter of time before companies that make this mistake discover that their hires can't cut it.

Elements of a great culture should remain constant as a company grows, and include the following:

- leaders who consistently live and reinforce company values.

- open communication without fear of retribution.

- opportunities for advancement.

- complete company transparency.

- engaged team members who take ownership of their roles.

- a clear company purpose.

RECOVERY FROM CULTURE SHOCK

I once worked in an ultra-competitive company culture wherein the leadership challenged employees by design. Team members competed for money, meaning if you got it somebody else might not. In most revenue-producing positions, healthy competition is a good thing both internally (within the company) and externally (with other companies), but never to the company's detriment. At this particular company, though, the employees (especially the sales team) would do practically anything to get by, so the body count was high. So high, that it stifled the company's growth. It was a profitable company but could have achieved even more if not for such an internally-competitive culture.

Years later, the owner told me he believed fierce competitiveness motivated employees and built businesses, and it's hard to argue with someone who experienced such amazing success. This culture increased the company's revenue and earnings, and it sold for a lot of money. They also grew successful leaders, arguably because of the culture.

Later in my career when it came time for me to take the reins at another company, I took what I learned from that experience—both good and bad—and promised myself I'd do it differently: bigger, and in half the time with happier people. Instead of that internal fight for dollars, my team fought external competition for sales, and salespeople could do well collectively. I frequently chose larger companies to target, and it was always satisfying to take a piece of the market from each of them. I developed a culture of trust, respect and intense focus, and employees appreciated my leadership and working in the safe, positive environment. That company went from $3 million to $30 million in nine years, which had taken the other company many more years to accomplish.

Overlooked Opportunities & Opinions

- Employees who feel they're managed in a motivating way: 21%.

- Employees who say they have the opportunity to do what they do best: 4 in 10.

- Employees who strongly agree their opinions count at work: 3 in 10.

(Source: Gallup)

CULTURE FAIL

One of the most famous examples of a corrupt culture is Enron. Enron's values (*integrity, communication, respect and excellence),* chiseled in marble in the lobby of its former Houston headquarters, weren't real. Enron's senior management failed to sustain transparency with company information and demonstrated little regard for ethics or their employees' needs.

Total transparency is vital for any winning organization or team. According to recent research, in fact, strong management transparency leads to 30% higher employee retention. Conversely, companies that aren't forthcoming, or that hide their numbers or indicators will face difficulty recruiting or retaining winners. It's hard to feel like part of a team when information is being kept from you.

Asking employees to affect the bottom line, or paying them to deliver net income when they have no control over expenses or revenue isn't right. When objectives are simply driven by management doling them out to employees (aka the *achieve this or you don't work here* mentality), people will still take the jobs because they need them, but they're done before they begin.

Hiding good news from employees is just as harmful. For example, some owners may downplay a successful year because they don't want employees to ask about their share in the way of raises or bonuses. This type of *reactive* leadership hopes to avoid exposure and the resulting conflict because it's likely their employees aren't being paid properly. The proactive and transparent leaders, however, are already compensating their people well and don't have employees who ask, "*Where's mine?*" They already got theirs. The bottom line on transparency: When leadership and/or management don't communicate regularly and openly, team members will either be forced to make up their own answers or leave for more transparent companies.

Be the Apple not the Enron

Apple is an example of a company that practices its values. I'm an Apple freak and become more of a fan every time I talk to a representative in any capacity. The employees address issues quickly, apparently empowered and prepared to offer solutions. It's a culture that ensures Apple customers enjoy the experience they have come to expect whenever they interact with any Apple representative in person, online or by phone. Apple's core values include making great, simple, easy-to-use products that are accessible by everyone, serving their customers better than anyone else, and not compromising their ethics or integrity in the name of profit. Whenever I have a bad customer service experience at a big company, I look up its value statement and then email the CEO. The great ones actually respond!

CHAPTER 4
Hiring Winners

Professional Help

Successful recruiting is a journey not a destination. It's also a learned process, which involves searching for and selecting the right people for the right jobs, and not settling. And, since there's a direct relationship between acquiring talented employees and the overall profits of a company, finding the correct fit has a lot riding on it.

Hiring great team members isn't easy, but companies that accept mediocrity are ultimately doomed. Without the great people, building great teams becomes a moot point. The good news is that it's possible to succeed the first time and find effective team members by following a recruitment plan.

The New Normal

The typical American hiring process used to go like this: write a job description, place an ad, receive resumes, interview every prospect, and then hire someone from the bunch. However, with so many advancements in technology, companies no longer have to accept less than they need.

Before the internet and social media, managers relied on job listings in the local newspaper or trade publications to recruit qualified professionals. Since the reach was limited to local applicants, managers either interviewed the same people again and again or had to hire someone who wasn't an exact match and sometimes not even a close match. Now, with the scope of the internet, it's never been easier to access qualified candidates, greatly increasing the chances of finding the perfect person for a particular position.

Just a decade ago, it wasn't unusual for candidates to be offered a job after only one interview but now that's rarely the case. Due to an increase in quality candidates, it's not uncommon to be interviewed three to five times by different people in the company before an offer is made. The type of employee being sought has shifted, too. Technical abilities matter and so does the right personality type. Hiring managers also want to know that the individuals they're recruiting are able to learn new skills and adapt to an always-changing business environment.

Now, not only do candidates have to prove themselves, but companies also have to sell themselves to quality people. Top candidates want to work for employers they can learn from.

They want to know what the company culture is like, and what values matter most to management. *Is it a collaborative office or is individual problem-solving valued? Is working from home permitted?*

According to Glassdoor (a website that lists employment opportunities, salary information and company reviews), job seekers read six reviews about a company before forming opinions, and 69% won't accept a job with a company that has a bad reputation. So, if a business' reputation is unfavorable on social media, people probably won't be clamoring to work there.

Negative reviews not only impact those applying for jobs, but also put off potential customers or clients, which cost companies in potential future revenue. Employers can't control social media and some websites have the ability to significantly influence opinions. A company could receive all the awards in the world, but if word gets out that it's a bad place to work or the leader is a jerk, that information goes global.

Management Must Mobilize

Recruitment training starts at the top and the CEO should be the company's best recruiter—this is one of the leadership team's most important roles. I once discussed hiring with a CEO whose company was shrinking instead of growing. He lamented the fact that everyone management hired was below par and the good ones left. After speaking with him, I concluded that he couldn't hire A players because he was a C leader.

A's don't work for C leaders.

Companies without charismatic leaders attracting top people will breed more uncharismatic and uninspiring leaders. This particular CEO needed to honestly reflect on the kind of example he set and ask himself how he expected his people to keep improving when he wasn't. That's why I advise young people beginning their careers to pick not only a great company to work for, but also a great leader. It'll be like getting a virtual MBA on the job.

While working on their own self-improvement plan, CEOs sometimes can overcome certain hurdles and shortcomings by hiring people with the strengths they're lacking. Apple and Microsoft, for instance, have that kind of culture. They employ people who supplement the leadership skills they lack. Still, their leaders had to first recognize their limitations and then agree to hiring those people with supplemental capabilities. I was often given equity roles because owners acknowledged their shortcomings and needed me to enhance those areas, where I excelled. Besides making sure revenue increased and implementing a plan that made money, one of my best attributes as a leader was recruiting great teams.

My ability to recruit came from Gary Anderson, who built Directors Mortgage Company, which was acquired for many hundreds of millions of dollars by a national bank. We were both members of a YPO (formerly Young Presidents' Organization) peer group, and he was the best recruiter I ever met. His company developed a two-pronged recruiting model that satisfied both the short- and long-term revenue needs of a business by building teams in two ways:

1. Immediate gratification by hiring freelance executives, trained elsewhere and available for the right opportunities.

2. Long-term growth by building a team internally, earning loyalty by providing training, a great culture and strong leadership.

Throughout my career, I've never paid a recruiter. What's more, I've met hundreds of CEOs from million—and even billion-dollar companies—and the majority of them never hired a game-changer through a recruiter. In fact, the ratio of recruiter hires being successful is in the low single digits. Additionally, recruiter fees are exorbitant—15-35% of the employee's first year's salary.

In my view, most (but not all) recruiters reprocess dissatisfied workers who are looking to escape positions where they're failing, not making enough money, or hate their bosses. They typically interview well because headhunters habitually send them to many companies. Recruiters can be helpful for highly-technical or specialized fields, such as top-end software engineers, scientists or nuclear physicists. However, if you're looking for salespeople and office managers, pass.

Rules of Recruitment

CEOs who followed a process and/or heeded my recruiting dos and don'ts below, found 90% of their great people that way. A word of caution—rushing through the hiring process compromises the quality of any team.

Recruiting Dos:

- **Develop a budget based on business goals, with a staffing/manpower component.** For example, if you want to increase your sales revenue by $1 million in the next year and your salespeople average $500,000 annually, hire two people prior to the year starting and give them time to train and ramp up their production. Expecting new hires to hit their goals right out of the gate will only serve to disappoint you. Ideally, the sales team sets graduated goals. Instead of simply setting an annual goal of $1 million, for example, managers should divide it into increasing quarterly goals: $100,000 the first quarter, $200,000 the second, $300,000 the third and $400,000 in the fourth. It's a stepladder toward success and, frankly, it's startling to me that many companies don't do it.

- **Craft a recruitment plan.** A recruitment plan pinpoints the job description and the skills and experience the company is seeking. It also addresses how the position will be publicized and lists the people who will provide input for the job description, review applications, participate in the interviews and make the final hiring decision.

- **Write a job description with employee input.** How do you hire someone if you're not exactly sure who you're looking for? That's why everyone who's going to be involved with the new hire should take part.

- **Recruit internally whenever possible.** Hiring internally is the best way to meet an organization's needs. Internal candidates are already familiar with the company's operation. They have built relationships with coworkers, may need less training and have a proven track record. Promoting and training up staff can be motivating for all employees, who will feel that their hard work is being recognized. It boosts not only morale but also productivity. It's a manager's responsibility to inform internal candidates that they're part of a group being interviewed and that if they're passed over, they'll identify why and develop an action plan together to help them qualify for upcoming positions.

- **Get employee referrals.** If no current employees are right for the job, the next best options are internal referrals. Employee referrals have the highest applicant-to-hire conversion rate by far. I once increased a team from eighty members to 300 and almost all of the new hires came from employee referrals.

  We'd developed a great culture, so our people referred their friends to us. Eagles hang out with other eagles.

- **Branch out to your network and centers of influence (COIs) with the position requirements.** COIs are your clubs, churches, schools, connections, nonprofits and business associates. Share the search with everyone you know and focus on only people that you source or are referred to.

- **Find someone who's already successful at another company in the position you're looking to fill.** The best people aren't actively seeking jobs and they're the ones you want to recruit into your culture.

- **Take advantage of free marketing through your networks and resources.** Besides sources previously mentioned, I use LinkedIn, Facebook, and supplier and customer referrals.

- **Create a recruitment database and reach out to prospects quarterly.** Whenever I identified a top performer from another company, I made sure to touch base with him or her quarterly—whether by email or phone to meet for coffee, golf or anything that kept us in contact. Good people don't jump ship easily, but circumstances inevitably change—companies are acquired, have financial difficulties, cut commissions or change leadership—and those coveted people will be ready to pursue other options. If you've kept in touch, guess who they'll call? (Once, I pursued a salesperson quarterly for nine years. Eventually, he worked for me and produced big numbers.)

- **Keep looking for people even when you think you're fully staffed.** Never stop recruiting. If you find someone more qualified than an existing employee, look for another spot for the person currently holding the position. Great people pay for themselves so I've never been afraid to bring an additional person to a team.

- **Award bonuses to all internal recruiters.** In the sales department, for instance, part of a manager's annual bonus should be based on how many *producing* salespeople they've hired. If the manager hires ten salespeople and only two are performing, then eight people were paid for nothing, so the bonus should reflect that.

Don't bother:

- **Placing ads in newspapers.** They're archaic remnants of the way business used to be done.

- **Hiring job hoppers.** These are people with several short-term jobs in their career histories, or people actively looking for jobs. Top performers rarely need to look for employment because opportunities and people (like me) find them.

- **Using recruiting software.** Recruiting software, like a headhunter, basically searches for people who are looking for work, and I generally prefer hiring those currently doing their jobs successfully.

- **Hiring fresh-out-of-college graduates without serious consideration.** Unless companies have great training programs, access to mentors, and the time and money to invest, taking chances on newbies could be a mistake. From the 1960s to the late 1990s, training was done regularly by many of the best companies but then seemed to decrease steadily.

- **Consulting market studies.** I've never seen a valid market study—primarily because the relevance depends largely on its participants. If, for example, a survey represents only salaries in large U.S. companies in different geographical locations, then it's not applicable for determining compensation in small local companies. Both employers and employees need to know the field and what competitors in the area pay by conducting their own surveys of the marketplace and similar businesses.

- **Hiring on instinct.** I've done it, and it never works out. The gut is effective when backed by process. However, unsupported instinct can be a disaster. Having a method for hiring, and sticking to it, will result in choosing more winners than losers. Owners of private businesses are particularly infamous for coming across the next company *savior* (or so they think) and forcing them upon a team. Invariably, the team immediately recognizes the *savior* is wrong for the job. It happens more than you might think.

Porsches Go Poof!

During the dotcom bubble of the 1990s, many senior executives asked for new Porsches as signing bonuses. I tried to educate them, and many listened, but those that chose to work for companies that offered the sports cars (or other unfeasible extravagances) found themselves unemployed when the tech bubble burst. (And sans Porsches because most of them were repossessed.) You can't compete with, or give into, unrealistic short term demands or expectations. Businesses pay what the market dictates over time.

Promotion Pitfalls

Although preferred, promoting internally does have its challenges—especially when the move is from team member to team leader. The reality is that top performers don't always make the best leaders. Even so, companies often promote employees because it's the easiest and quickest solution (e.g. advancing the biggest sales producer to the VP of sales). At first, the promoted employee is enamored with their new office and title, however, it's usually a disaster for both the company and the new leader.

The qualities and behaviors that drove results in sales aren't transferable to leading. Sales leaders are often egocentric and unable to function in a team environment. Other than putting up big numbers, the boss-like attributes end there.

It's hard to fathom, but a former NBA superstar didn't fare well transitioning from player to general manager and then owner. Like in the corporate world, the two positions involve completely different skill sets and being good at one doesn't guarantee success in the other.

Making matters worse, there's usually no training on how to do the job correctly. Before long, these misplaced leaders realize they're expected to work longer hours, train people and relinquish control of their income (relying instead on others who aren't top producers). Whenever I see a company promote someone to the CEO role mainly because that person has been at the company for a long time, I worry it's not going to end well.

The greatest managers or leaders have studied their crafts, work hard and have strong processes in place. The money may be better selling, but there are many incredible people who don't want to be on the sales treadmill (solely dependent on production forever) and opt to normalize their income instead. These are the people who make good leaders.

A Job Description Tutorial

After compiling input from everyone involved with the position to be filled, it's time to write the job description. The following template will help those who are in charge of hiring collect the information necessary for finding the right person.

Job title:

State official job title.

Compensation range and benefits:

It's important for people to understand how they'll get paid and promoted, and how they will receive benefits. Whenever I recruit I explain that unless employees take on other roles in the company, their salaries remain the same, no matter how long they stay. What changes are the performance bonuses that are awarded when they exceed their goals.

It's important for both employers and employees to keep current on what *real-world* compensation levels look like. I've interviewed people for key positions who use salary studies of Fortune 500 companies as the benchmarks for their compensation. A sales director for a $20-million company will never make the same money as a sales director for a $2-billion company. Likewise, a billion-dollar company looking for a human resources VP to manage 300 people will undoubtedly pay more than a $50-million company looking for an equivalent candidate to manage two people. Budgets and needs determine levels of compensation. (Reality must be observed at all times.)

Skills needed to perform in the position:

Be specific.

Major goals and responsibilities:

Briefly describe the purpose of the job and the result if it's done well. List basic measurable goals with responsibilities in order of importance and timeframes.

Managers will establish and measure activity- and behavior-related, short-term goals for the first 90 days of employment. For example, new hires will learn a sales presentation and deliver it to the team, or make a predetermined number of new account calls to be entered into a Customer Relationship Management (CRM) system (which manages future and current client/customer interactions).

Essential activities:

List the five most important daily activities of the position in order of importance, and the percentage of time that should be spent on each.

Task list:

List current projects with completion dates in order of importance.

People managed:

If applicable, include direct and indirect people who the new hire will report to, along with their titles and summary of duties. There might also be people who report to the new hire, so leadership must make sure he or she is capable of managing them.

Primary contacts:

Identify those people with whom the person in this position will deal with on a daily basis, both internal and external.

Challenges of the job:

Describe the biggest challenges that may hamper success in this position. Hiring managers need to make sure that an applicant's skills and behaviors are equal to all the tasks they will face.

Review process:

Include when it happens and by whom. This should be a circular process with confidential feedback from all parties involved with the new hire. A 360° performance review enables team members and other managers to provide objective input on an employee's performance, skills, work habits and overall effectiveness and is especially helpful during a trial period.

Interviewing: The Q & A Portion of the Program

INTERVIEWING INSIGHT

By the time a candidate is brought in for an interview, the people in charge of hiring should be fairly certain that he or she would be able to perform the job responsibilities. They should also have a good idea about how the candidate's abilities align not only with the position, but also with the organization. The interview provides confirmation of whether or not a candidate is likely to succeed in a particular job. If 1,000 resumes come in and no one fulfills the established requirements, then no one should be interviewed.

Interviews are conducted by the hiring manager and at least two other employees who have been trained to recognize all the qualities candidates need to be positive team additions. Why three interviewers? To me, three represents a quorum. Two never seems to be enough and can often result in a deadlock.

We all have biases within our own disciplines, so I prefer one interviewer to be from outside of the department that the new hire will be joining. Having varied thinking styles involved in decision-making improves the odds of a positive outcome. I like someone in finance or operations to be the third person in any sales hires since those departments will regularly interact with the person in that position. I think having HR departments run interviews for senior positions is a waste of time unless the department heads are extremely talented. Otherwise, most people don't know how to conduct proper interviews.

Finally, interviewers have only two choices: **yes** or **no**. If any ONE of the three interviewers votes no after meeting with a candidate, then he or she is out of the running. Someone is hired only when candidates receive *three yeses*—one from each interviewer. **Maybe** is a no. People hire maybes all the time and then are surprised when they fail. If you have doubts about any aspect of a person before hiring, they'll multiply after.

PRE-GAME WARM-UPS

I'm often asked to do the final interviews of people being considered for jobs. Before meeting candidates, no matter the position they're applying for, I always assign small tasks, something to see who's seriously interested in the job. For example, I contact prospects and ask them to email me with days and times that they're available to speak that week. After scheduling a day, the next assignment will be to call me at the designated time.

I'm looking for behaviors that illustrate candidates are making every timely effort to secure the position. What I love is when someone calls me two minutes early or emails first thing in the morning to confirm our call later that day. Even those simple actions provide further clues of what I can expect if I hire them—or if I want to interview someone at all.

I interview prospects in a focused, one-on-one setting that is free from interruptions or distractions. I'm not a fan of group interviews because there's always a dominant personality (typically the senior leader) who takes over or derails the process. Basically, whatever he thinks becomes what everybody thinks, aka Groupthink. Groupthink occurs when individual members unquestioningly follow the leader, and the group discourages dissent from the consensus. In other words, people usually won't speak up and oppose the boss.

I want interviewees to feel comfortable, so I don't typically sit behind the king's desk. Instead, I sit with candidates at a table or on a couch, so it feels relaxed and more like a discussion than a formal interview. I also make note when an applicant arrives and take it seriously whenever someone's late. In most cases, tardiness disqualifies them.

Some companies routinely ask sales candidates to do presentations for the sales team and then team members offer feedback to the hiring manager. As a result, those companies experience minimal turnover and their salespeople succeed. Typically, I have applicants vying for sales, marketing or senior executive roles give presentations on chosen subjects to management, the sales team or the three interviewers. For example, if I'm hiring a CFO I might ask him or her to present on the steps necessary to raise $3 million in capital. Serious contenders show up over-prepared, and sometimes the people a company had high hopes for come in and bomb.

LEADING QUESTIONS

I want to hire people who are not only smart, team-oriented and competitive, confident and skilled, but who have also exhibited fortitude in the face of adversity—a crucial trait in top employees. Without these attributes, a person doesn't have a shot at working for me. If candidates aren't being interviewed for revenue-generating positions, then they are overhead, and better be brilliant team players.

I employ behavioral interviewing, based on the assumption that past behavior is the best predictor of future behavior. It's also a method used to aid interviewers in discovering what really drives a candidate, not just what they've done. The questions are designed to obtain insights into someone's experience, skills, knowledge, and behaviors beyond what can be found on a resume. Learning how candidates acted in past work situations, interviewers can get a good indication of how they'll act in the new position.

I begin interviews by asking candidates about their high school years. Traits, such as a strong work ethic, are formed by the first grade and early formative experiences (like high school) help shape someone's moral compass. Whether recruits come from backgrounds of little money or third-generation wealth, interviewers will find high school presidents, honor students and star athletes are well-rounded, driven people whose behaviors for success formed when they were young.

The three interviewers should be prepared with a list of pre-approved questions. Following are examples along with explanations of what the answers may reveal about candidates. (Interviewers should always push for real, reflective answers.)

1. **Why did you leave your previous jobs?** How many jobs did they have in the past five years, and what reasons do they give? Do candidates have valid explanations, such as the company was sold or the owner's son took over, or just excuses?

2. **What is your greatest business or personal accomplishment?** I don't let candidates get away with hurried, shallow answers, or tell me about some sales awards they received. I'm looking for events they consider to be true triumphs in their lives and I give them time to think about it. The serious candidates dig deep.

    I once posed this question to a young man interviewing for a finance position. He answered that getting his finance degree was hard because he had to work full-time to pay for school. It took him six years, but he was proud of his achievement and said he planned to teach those values to his future children someday. That's the sort of response I'm seeking.

3. **Describe the best manager you've ever had and why you liked working for him or her?** Pay attention to the qualities that made an impression and helped the person succeed. Is the company's management style similar to what the candidate is used to? This information will help further assess position compatibility.

4. **How weird are you on a scale of one to five?** Candidates who choose one or two may be a little too straight-laced for certain company cultures, and a five may indicate someone is too unique or unconventional for others to work well with.

5. **How lucky are you in life on a scale of one to five?** According to the experts, candidates who rate themself as a one may not know why bad things happen to them and have tendencies to blame others. If they're a five, they may have high expectations and always look at every outcome as positive.

6. **In one word, how would you describe yourself?** The word isn't as important as the insight into how people package themselves.

7. **What would I hear if I asked an eclectic group of people who know you for three adjectives that best describe you?**

   The group of people include:

   - the candidate's food delivery guy.
   - former coworker.
   - least favorite boss.
   - favorite teacher.
   - high school nemesis.

   Do the candidates' opinions of themselves match the interviewers' impressions?

8. **How old were you when you had your first paying job?** I look for a deeply instilled work ethic and try to weed out any hint of entitlement. Working part-time during high school and college shows a huge level of personal responsibility, for instance.

   One day, a neighbor's 8-year-old kid went door to door peddling "really cool crystals" to raise money for a bike. I gave him $5 for basically a bunch of rocks from his backyard that he was hawking as if they were diamonds. Coming from privilege didn't prevent him from understanding the concept that if you want money, you have to go out and make it. These kinds of kids usually grow up to be the people I want on my team.

9. **What motivates you to get out of bed in the morning?** It's important to understand what drives and inspires candidates.

10. **If we were sitting here a year from now, celebrating what a great year it's been for you in this role, what did we achieve together?** The candidate should have enough strategic vision to not only talk about how good the year has been, but also answer with a bigger-picture understanding in terms of the company.

11. **What's the biggest misperception people have about you?** The answer reveals a candidate's level of self-awareness.

12. **Can you tell me about a time when you almost gave up, how you felt about that, and how you persevered?** Great people figure out how to continually succeed even under difficult circumstances. There will always be ups and downs in any business, and it's important that potential employees will be equally motivated during the difficult times—if not more so. Leaders lean toward things where the stakes are relatively high, the dynamics are complex and teamwork matters, and it's important that they hire employees who'll do the same.

After the last question, I wrap up the interview by asking candidates if there's anything else they'd like to explain that wasn't disclosed on their resumes before our thorough due diligence. You never know what you may uncover. For example, did they omit a three-month job or a lengthy hiatus between jobs?

"I had another job but didn't include it because I got fired."

I hear that a lot. Occasionally, candidates leave off something that could make them more valuable for positions.

"I was working on a contract basis and thought short-term might look bad."

However, an interim job outside their industries as a cashier or bartender while waiting for the right permanent position, shows responsibility as opposed to being unemployed during that time.

An Alternate Route

In several cities and states, it's no longer legal to ask about salary history as part of the interviewing process. The banning of the question is part of the efforts to ensure pay equity for women. People in favor of the ban believe that determining future compensation based on unfair lower salaries only perpetuates wage inequality. Opposition points to statistics, such as this one from HireRight's 2017 employment screening benchmark report that says 85% of employers caught applicants fibbing on their resumes or applications, up from just 66% five years ago. Salespeople particularly are notorious for taking their biggest month ever and multiplying by 12 to come up with their previous (and imaginary) salaries.

In the meantime, employers must find ways to validate performance. For example, interviewers should ask sales candidates about revenue that they produced the previous year, rather than income. Or, what was the budget or performance goal and what percentage did they reach with each? Instead of asking what they got paid, I ask how. I want people that received salary and bonuses and made their targets.

References: A Reality Check

Following the interview and the pre-offer, checking the references, background, educational and employment history of candidates is the last step before the formal offer. I ask finalists to provide three references who can talk about their characters and abilities, and the reasons why they chose them. I give them the days that I'm available and then they're responsible for setting up the calls. This way, I'm not chasing people who may not want to talk, in which case, I get my answers anyway. If former employers or managers refer to employment laws or are skittish about talking to future employers or their representatives, then they don't have anything good to say.

The reality is that because of the litigious state of business, most HR departments will only answer questions regarding dates of employment and eligibility for rehire. They're subject to rules and regulations that prevent significant conversations regarding potential applicants so they're not especially helpful to employers. Candidates who performed well and left on amicable terms won't have any trouble getting former managers or employers to share those experiences. Lastly, employers should check public social media profiles and posts to confirm they're hiring the people they've gotten to know.

One of the best people I ever hired for a sales position was fresh out of Berkeley. In this particular company we had a great training program and two mentors who also were part of the hiring process. I asked the candidate for references from a professor and her boss at the bookstore where she worked, and I heard from both of them that night. That told me they were eager to talk, which is always a good sign.

Every now and then I've been compelled to answer "no comment" to reference calls myself, which I'm well aware speaks volumes. I once declined to discuss a candidate with a manager, who was particularly caught off guard by my refusal since it'd taken the company 90 days to find him. My non-response prompted the hiring company's further investigation and discovery that the candidate had been fired from three jobs in five years.

Interestingly, the hiring company's CEO held three degrees but was never trained in how to recruit or interview. He had constant turnover of sales and marketing people because frankly, he hired losers. I remember asking that same CEO why one particular manager he'd recently hired left his last job. He told me the guy had been promised ownership and when he didn't get it he left. I had to break it to him that the guy's former company was a family business and equity to anybody outside of the family was never an option. That was news to the CEO.

Know How to Hold 'Em: Employee Retention

MIS-HIRES, TURNOVERS AND COSTS, OH, MY!

What good is hiring superstars if you can't keep them? The U.S. Bureau of Labor Statistics reports that three million employees have left their jobs voluntarily every month since June 2017 and Gallup estimates that millennial turnover due to poor engagement costs the U.S. economy $30.5 billion a year.

One of the most effective ways to ease the burden of turnover is by preventing it in the first place. Employers must understand what drives employee behavior and foster a positive, engaging work environment where employees do their best work and want to stick around. To that end, management and employees must keep the lines of communication open. Employees who feel comfortable with their leaders are more engaged and inspired.

Companies can also reduce turnover by concentrating on employee personal growth and development, and by paying good people what they're worth (instead of making it easy for competitors to swoop in and lure them away). Offering remote work programs is another way companies get people to stick around since a large majority of working Americans want to work remotely at least part of the time. Companies that support remote working arrangements report 25% lower employee turnover than companies that don't. Finally, experts cite the need to fill positions quickly as the main reason that bad hires are made, so spending more time up front and not rushing the process will save employers money and time in the end.

I worked with the CEO of a high-growth business that had sixteen of twenty new hires leave in the prior year. We revamped his hiring process—and by revamp, I mean we started from scratch with the recruitment and interviewing steps previously mentioned. His team hired fourteen people the following year who were all still with him at the end of the next, and the company's revenue soared. Lazy hiring practices are bad hiring practices. You cannot do just one thing to counteract bad hiring and ongoing turnover, you have to do *everything* right to balance the impact of it.

Low or no turnover is also a problem, most likely indicating other underlying issues. It may signal a poor HR department, an inadequate hiring process, the absence of a career path within the company or weak management that slacks on regularly reviewing progress—which also means that dreaded complacency has set in. Some turnover is healthy, but a company can't have high-performance if the detrimental underperformers never leave. According to Gallup, turnover rates shouldn't surpass 10% in great companies.

MORE FACTS TO TURN OVER

- According to the Harvard Business Review, as much as 80% of employee turnover is due to bad hiring decisions.

- The successful aren't immune from having to learn from their hiring mistakes. Zappos CEO Tony Hsieh once estimated that his own bad hires cost the company well over $100 million.

- The largest 100 companies in the world admit that only 20% of the people they hire turn out to be high performers who fit their culture—that's only one out of five.

- Studies also show that approximately 20% of employee turnover happens in the first 90 days of employment.

- Cost estimates of losing employees vary based on multiple factors, including the positions vacated. For example, research suggests that replacing highly-trained employees and executives can cost more than double the annual salary of the role.

- A bad hire costs not only money, but also time and effort invested in hiring and rehiring.

TRAINING PREVENTS TURNOVER

Training is a worthwhile investment for any company and a huge factor in preventing turnover. Yet, the vast majority of businesses today lack defined development programs, and if they have them, most are inadequate. Organizations without training programs don't have capable, promotable workers on deck to replace non-performers when they go. Instead, they pay for talent currently employed elsewhere. However, if companies are simply the highest bidders for these *hired guns* and don't invest in training them into their cultures and offering long-term career paths, the new hires will be replaced by the next group of hired guns or move onto greener pastures elsewhere.

In hockey, there's a great deal of time, money and resource devoted to continual training and I applied the same emphasis on training in business. Growth is the goal for most businesses, and the companies that invest in long-term development of employees create a stable, loyal, and committed workforce which results in more opportunity and financial reward in the end. Additionally, there are state and federal tax programs that are readily available to employers to offset the cost of training and hiring.

THAT'LL TEACH 'EM

A solid employee development program is also considered a benefit in the hiring package which gives companies a competitive edge over others without formal training programs. Businesses that care enough to provide training, entice potential employees who continually want to improve and keep up with field progress. In turn, hiring managers seek out these desirable employees.

Training Truths:

- Research shows that 40% of employees who don't receive the necessary job training will leave their positions within the first year.*

- Companies with less than one hundred employees only average twelve minutes of management training every six months. Companies with 100-500 employees receive a measly six minutes of management training every six months.*

- Businesses investing $1,500 or more per employee annually on training average 24% higher profit margins than companies with lower annual training budgets; they also generate a 6% higher shareholder return if the training expenditure per employee increases by $680. (Source: The American Society for Training and Development)

- Employment of training and development specialists is projected to grow 11% from 2016 to 2026, faster than the average for all occupations.*

(*source: Bureau of Labor Statistics)

SLOW TO HIRE... QUICK TO FIRE

Even after properly recruiting and training, companies can make mistakes. It happens, and in those unfortunate cases, managers shouldn't waste time defending how it happened but should act quickly and cut their losses. The swifter they act, the easier the process will be for both parties. Chances are the employees have seen the writing on the wall too—or more specifically, on their scorecards—and know what's coming. Managers who spend a significant amount of time considering firing bad hires, should have already done it. Companies that waffle suffer far-reaching consequences, including negative effects on employee morale, culture and leadership—all resulting in decreased sales.

During a typical probation period, employees aren't eligible for benefits such as vacation and paid time off, but after that they'll most likely be on the employers' ticket for unemployment. So, whenever possible, managers should make changes within 90 days. New hires that have been reviewed regularly and actively managed during trial periods should already know that being hired after probation isn't guaranteed.

On those occasions when termination becomes necessary, managers must always be legally and morally compliant and do so in a professional manner. It's never a good idea to fire someone on a whim either; people should be allowed to leave with dignity even when management may feel that they don't deserve it. Losing it never helps, and just gives the terminated employees power. Employers should pay severance, get a release and resist getting indignant or angry in order to avoid challenges like a lawsuit. Once the legal system gets involved, you'll realize that's the wrong way to handle things.

WELCOME NEW HIRES

How new employees are welcomed lays the groundwork for whether or not they'll hang around for long. Ideally, managers keep in touch with new employees from the time they accept the job and begin building relationships right away. Still, the first day sets a tone and having everything ready for new hires to do their jobs is the best way to start any employment. It's management's responsibility to announce the hiring of new employees and plan the onboarding process. Employees who feel at ease from the start will be motivated to perform. Whenever possible, I like to hire in pairs. Pairs feed off each other and do things together. Training is also twice as effective.

On day one, new hires should have their 90-day plan that includes scheduled times for proper onboarding, training and integration in general, and be assigned mentors, preferably company cheerleaders at the same job level. Disgruntled or unhappy coworkers tend to quickly attach themselves to newbies since failure (like misery) prefers company. A prearranged lunch for new hires with their teams or the people they report to should be mandatory, and some kind of welcome package is a nice touch.

> **Experts cite poor onboarding experience and a lack of clarity surrounding job duties and expectations among top reasons why employees leave jobs.**

On my first day in a management role for a large company, my manager was out of town and no one was expecting me. Although I'd been hired the month before, no one bothered to schedule an HR appointment for me so the director didn't have a clue who I was. As a result, I didn't have a computer, printer, an email address or business cards. That was my welcome to my new job. In the first hour of that new job I thought, *What am I doing here?* Studies have shown that the first month of a new hire or assignment is critical to the overall success of that employee's tenure with the organization.

My manager, although a good one, knew nothing about the onboarding process. He just didn't get it. So, after a week, I decided to onboard myself. I asked for a company directory and consulted the top salespeople, who apparently had suffered the same hiring experience. It was an unfortunate cultural thing. Nevertheless, what I wanted to know is how these salespeople became successful and I peppered them with questions about their process. Following their suggestion, I picked one hundred key accounts to pursue, began calling them and succeeded quickly. Had I waited for the company to get me started, however, I would have missed out on a month of hefty commissions. That's how I discovered the bigger the company, the worse the onboarding process.

CHAPTER 5
Keeping Score

The Scoreboard Never Lies

SPECIAL MEASURES

I attended my first of many Chicago Blackhawk games in-utero as my pregnant mom cheered on the star goaltender, aka my dad. Looking back, I'm convinced my drive to win was as predestined as my hazel eyes. (It just took me over three decades to believe it.)

No matter the game or the opponents, the Rollins family always kept score. We competed with everything we had, and as a young boy I thought that if you could win in our yard or basement you could win anywhere. The Centennial Athletic Awards Programme, offering Canadian youth recognition for outstanding physical performance in events like running, sit-ups and push-ups, marked my first measurement or "scorecard" beyond school. Results were compared to other students throughout the city and province. I'm sure that scorecard is what planted the seeds for the ones I later used faithfully in the business world.

I loved that the challenge was a physical one and became manic about being the best in something I knew I'd be good at. Winners were awarded badges and wore them with pride. I remember it well because I trounced my competitors in every category and simultaneously had an epiphany: being measured against others was a rush, and receiving rewards and recognition was lots of fun.

IF YOU DON'T KEEP SCORE, WHY PLAY?

It's hard to imagine sports without scores. Scores play equally important parts in business and life, especially when it comes to setting any kind of goal. For instance, if you're on a diet but don't keep score, or track progress, how would you know when you reached your ideal weight? In other words, if you don't know where you are, how will you know where you're going or when you arrive?

Champions in all walks of life thrive on measurement and keeping score. Being aware of the stats helps people stay motivated, try harder and be constantly aware of what they must do to excel. There's no denying the truth of the scoreboard. Just like the parents of the junior sports phenoms who never complain that there's no place for scores (or trophies) in youth athletics, it's no surprise that it's the low performers in business who dislike being measured against their peers. Most people keep score only until they fail once and then quit, which is why most diets don't last long. Both successful dieters and employees, however, learn what's needed to improve.

THE ANATOMY OF A SCORECARD

When people actually see their performance toward goals, they can connect their behaviors with what's needed to win. Otherwise, it's out of sight, out of mind. Used as a management tool, a scorecard is like a job description with crystal clear accountabilities, such as targets and related key metrics, and displays regularly-tracked progress in time-bound increments.

Key metrics, also known as key performance indicators (KPIs), are a fundamental part of the scorecard used for employee evaluation, and are critical to a company's success. They're quantifiable measurements for assessing the status of specific deadline-driven processes or predetermined goals of companies, departments and employees, from the top-level down. KPIs motivate employees to perform better and attain higher ratings which, in turn, improve the business as a whole. When scorecards are presented to employees in black and white, consistently tracked and recorded, managers and employees always know the scores.

Since KPIs are based on position, experience, education and ability, team member involvement in determining those key metrics is vital. That's also why one employee's scorecard will differ from another's. Not all employees are created equal, so applying the same rules for all employees even in the same department isn't appropriate. Along with having regular access to scorecards, all team members must also understand:

- the categories in which they'll be rated.
- the time period covered.
- the grading system.
- the part scores play in their overall evaluations.
- the ways to improve ratings.

Just like I ultimately devised my own business plan, I also created a business scorecard from the best of what I learned from others, which I modify to suit each company's particular needs. I assess a company's last three years in these categories:

- Revenue
- Net income
- Growth (percentage)
- SG & A (selling, general and administrative expenses) or operating costs
- Some type of rating/grading for tracking both employee and client retention

Salespeople, the easiest to measure, should be scored on obtaining new business and sales goals, and their sales numbers shared via the company network, too. Along with quarter-to-date (QTD) and year-to-date (YTD), month-to-date (MTD) is a necessary category to include on their scorecards. They also need financial incentives attached to getting new clients and increasing client retention. Salespeople choose to be the revenue producers and are the last people who should be able to hide from constant measurement—or the results.

Managers are responsible for getting underperformers up to budget and need a tracking system and budgeted headcount to maintain with a production quotient built into it. Companies can assess managers by finding the benchmark. For example, if a company has ten managers who average 8% turnover but an outlier, an obvious area of discrepancy, reveals that one manager is averaging 30%, leadership needs to examine why.

I always tie employees' goals to things they can influence. Employees are either part of the topline (revenues or gross sales) or the bottom line (overhead) and can control a number of things to some degree. Even employees who don't put up numbers should still be accountable to key metrics. Hourly or general line employees can control job performance, absenteeism, showing up on time, staying late when necessary, improvement and more.

Customer service employees should be scored on client retention and resolution of customer issues. They need training to follow a defined escalation process, and procedures to handle potential problems in different circumstances.

There's also the subjective part of it, such as employee attitudes. To help me assess this, I have each department score its coworkers in a blind evaluation to see who's going above and beyond. A good employee who really cares is just as valuable as a revenue-producing employee. My mother is a great example. Starting out in an entry-level position in collections for a large business in Canada, she had a good leader who inspired his team members to act as if they were owners, and she really behaved like one. Although she certainly wasn't being paid a fortune in those days, she was always dedicated to her responsibilities. (See a sample business scorecard in the Resource section.)

SURVEY THE SCORE

Businesses have to monitor not only their employees, but also their customers. After all, without customers—particularly happy ones—employees don't need to be assessed because they'll be out of jobs. The simplest way to determine customer satisfaction is to go directly to the source and ask about it. When customers share their experiences of a company, they are helping to make the business better.

Just like internal surveys reveal pertinent information regarding employees, external customer surveys identify the most important data—why people buy from a company and even more importantly, why they don't. CEOs who want to continue to improve their business must measure customer feedback since people are more concerned than ever about how they spend their time and money. Those answers provide the key to business survival.

The best time to conduct a satisfaction survey is when the experience is fresh in a customer's mind. Responses may be less accurate if businesses wait because it's easy to forget details over time. Therefore, customer/client surveys must be emailed soon after customer interactions with company personnel.

The frequency of customer satisfaction surveys depends on the frequency with which the company interacts with its customers.

Surveys, tracked to the employees who assisted in each case, help management assess performance. To get the best results, surveys should never have more than five questions, according to Fred Galloway, a professor and former associate dean and director of strategic programs in the School of Leadership and Education Sciences at University of San Diego. Instead of the usual one to ten scoring that gives answers with too wide a variance, he suggests that with a narrower one to five scoring spectrum the results are much more telling.

Additionally, SurveyMonkey.com, a survey platform for consumer and employee feedback, suggests that Net Promoter Scores (NPS) that measure customer experience and brand perception, and predict business growth are the simplest to send, understand and evaluate. The NPS asks only one question of customers: *How likely is it that customers will recommend the company/product/service to a friend or colleague?* NPS not only determines a customer's willingness to recommend, but also pinpoints exactly why he or she is or isn't willing to do so.

By using SurveyMonkey.com or Galloway's scoring system and NPS, companies can get a good read on customer experience. The most important factor in customer service is still direct contact. Having available, responsive company representatives answering customer queries in real time remains the best way to retain clients. All calls should be recorded and reviewed in a timely fashion.

Businesses take heed:

- After one negative experience, 51% of customers will never do business with that company again. (source: Newvoicemedia.com)

- Americans tell an average of 15 people about a poor service experience, versus the 11 people they'll tell about a good experience.*

- As a group, millennials are willing to spend an additional 21% for great customer care.*

(*source: American Express 2017 Customer Service Barometer)

The Winning Card

Salespeople rarely report lost sales, but I always tracked them. Anytime a member of my salesforce lost a deal to another company, he or she would have to bring me the business cards of the winning salespeople in exchange for $100. Then, I'd call the winners and inform them that they kicked the butts of my best salespeople and for that reason I want to learn from them. I've had very few people refuse me a lunch or a coffee, and I hired many great salespeople that way.

ALL KEYED UP WITH METRICS

Paddy Ginnell, my coach on the Flin Flon Bombers juniors team and a former player, had a plan tied to effective individual and team key metrics. The Bombers were always contenders because every one of us knew our roles and metrics and executed a plan more precisely and relentlessly than most teams we faced.

Whereas business team members get KPIs related to things such as sales goals, annual revenue and growth, players on my junior league team received KPIs regarding the following:

1. **Shots on goal.** Like the great Gretzky said, "You miss 100% of the shots you don't take."

2. **Hits.** Opposing players don't play well on their backsides.

3. **Giveaways.** Errors could result in the other team scoring.

Before each period, we were assigned our KPIs and knew we'd be constantly measured. Defensemen like me were measured more for our hits and lack of giveaways, but the skilled forwards owned the key metric of shots on goal. My hockey teammates, like my business coworkers, had to believe that hitting their individual targets also prompted meaningful achievement for the team.

BEYOND MEASURE

A few of my favorite apps that I use regularly to track progress include:

- Apple Watch or Fitbit for personal fitness
- Evernote for business and personal tasks and notes

- Microsoft To Do for business and personal to-dos

SUCCESS BY NUMBERS

It always comes down to numbers. By using simple metrics, Paddy Ginnell and his teams won at least 65% of the time during the years I followed them. In sports, if you win 65% of your games, your team lands in the playoffs every year.

SPORT	Total Games/Regular season	65% Wins/points	Make Playoffs
NFL	16	10.4 wins	88% + chance
NBA	82	53.3 wins	95% + chance
NHL	82	53.3/106.6	100%
MLB	162	105.3 wins	100%

Not only does that 65% statistic apply to sports across the board, but also to business and competing for customers in the market. When tracking qualified (see: real) prospects, salespeople who maintain a 65% winning record will be successful in business. That's just a bit above average. In general, where salespeople and businesses fail is when they track results of suspects, or unqualified prospects, versus qualified ones.

The ABCs of Topgrading

MAKING THE GRADE

After employees are assigned their key metrics, they must develop and progress to stay on their teams just like athletes.

To assess employees, I use a technique called *Topgrading*, from a book by the same name, developed by internationally renowned management psychologist Brad Smart Ph.D. Topgrading can also be utilized for evaluating job candidates, but I employ it primarily for internal evaluations.

The Topgrading system offers management a complete picture of a subject's personality, strengths and weaknesses, which can help companies avoid the costly mistake of hiring or keeping employees who aren't right for the jobs. I've met with managers who hadn't a clue how to evaluate employees because they didn't have the necessary data. This system allows them to make more informed decisions.

Topgrading is done in pro and college sports all the time. Athletes have to prove themselves every day, week, month and year. In business, Topgrading is a perpetual process too, and works at all employment levels. It ensures employees don't get parked at desks just taking up space. The best companies I know do it every two months, which I recommend.

The complete Topgrading system is outlined in Smart's many books on this topic, but I tend to simplify everything into bite-sized nuggets of information. I think when processes go too deep and require too much involvement, people don't do it. Instead, when using Topgrading, I grade in only two categories:

1. Abilities/performance
2. Attitudes/behaviors

Using grades A, B and C, I rate each employee in both groups.

In any industry, retaining great players takes effort. Managers unwilling to do the heavy lifting of continuous improvement on an ongoing basis are company problems. In any business, the biggest hindrance are leaders who compromise on the high-performance standard. I've seen too many organizations put up with people who earn A's in ability/performance but C's in attitude/behavior. They need to pay better attention to this and make changes at the top before they expect improvements throughout the company.

Up to Grade

Major companies using the Topgrading system include: General Electric, Barclays, American Heart Association, Honeywell, Lincoln Financial and Argo.

SHOOT FOR THE STARS

I want to have as many people with As in both ability/performance and attitude/behaviors as possible—but especially in management roles. The ratio of A to B and C players on a team directly correlates to a business' success or failure. Great companies build teams with A players.

A players on average make up 16% of a company's workforce and are the stars on teams. They're at the top of the talent available for the position at the compensation a budget allows. These are the team members that employers search for, and the employees most likely to leave a company for other opportunities if leadership doesn't do everything necessary to keep them.

A Player attributes:

- consistently performs above expected levels
- disciplined
- principled
- thinks like an owner

B players are important to companies since they're the largest group of an average workforce, accounting for 65%. Bs can be divided into three categories. The top 10% (if you're lucky!) are on their way up to As. Most of the Bs (about 40% of them) are the steady performers who always deliver, but don't have inspirations to move up or seek out opportunities for growth. The remaining 15% may be talented, but just don't care enough to make improvements and could drop to Cs if they're not constantly monitored and measured.

B Player attributes:

- reliable (but require more guidance than As)
- content being team players and don't desire the pressure or demands of A-type roles
- do the job you ask, but rarely go beyond that

C players make up the remaining 15% and are the employees that kill companies. It has been my experience that without aggressive development and management assistance, very few Cs ever move up to Bs, and it's the exception when it occurs—the overwhelming majority will eventually go away. The key is to not select Cs.

C Player attributes:

- unmotivated
- challenge and question management
- make excuses for not achieving results
- bring down the morale of others

Before firing Cs, managers must first try to figure out how to fulfill their responsibilities to underperformers by categorizing them and discerning where training is needed. Some Cs require guidance and an opportunity to elevate their games, so management needs a three- to six-month improvement plan in place. Then if goals aren't achieved, Cs need to be replaced. Employees are Cs often because managers didn't do their jobs either. Managers who have an abundance of Cs on their teams, should be evaluated, too.

Accountability: Recognizing the Score

IN THE BOOKS

In sports you can't hide from scores. They're printed in newspapers, posted online and appear indelibly in the record books and stat sheets for everyone to see. In hockey, like all sports, keeping score was done for us regularly. At the end of each period we'd go into the locker room and get our stats. Years later, I can look back, but I can't invent tales about being a great player because I wasn't—the proof is there, in black and white. My father was a phenomenal player and that irrefutable truth also remains eternally in the record books. The numbers always held us accountable, and by applying and building that same concept into each business culture, I didn't permit employees to hide either. I expected all members of every team from the mailroom to the corner office to be accountable for their roles.

Too often, I go into private companies where progress isn't repeatedly assessed. There's no expectation or accountability for anybody, and the all-too-common dialogue goes something like this:

> Me: When do you get financials?
>
> CEO: Whenever they're put on my desk.
>
> Me: When's that?
>
> CEO: It could be a different time every month.

Good companies have financials in by the tenth day following the month that just closed, average companies by the fifteenth, and after that the person responsible should be fired. The manager has to be held accountable too for not staying on top of this.

These days, accountability has become a dirty word. Managers don't want to ask employees to be accountable for fear of ruining a fun workplace or being the bad guy. To winners though, a fun workplace is a consistently successful business where people can make more money, learn and improve every day. The good news is that people who have a problem with accountability will sooner or later deselect themselves under a focused, efficient system.

HOME IS WHERE THE HEAT IS

At one company, I managed seventy salespeople and implemented the *Winner's Circle*. Every quarter, salespeople vied to qualify for a big annual trip. A monthly mailer sent home shared not only who was in contention for the trip, but also revealed everyone's stacked rankings—those above budget and those below. I don't think people really ever grow up and this was my version of a pseudo-report card going home to mom and dad.

In full disclosure, the trip was a way for peers and family members to recognize the scores. It'd been designed to kick the nonperformers out of bed in the morning or perhaps influence them to take fewer vacations and make changes instead of avoiding problems until they escalated. I hired MBAs who had the education and the tools, but they didn't go to work every day.

Most significant others of the low-scorers had no idea that their loved ones were struggling. They assumed things were fine until the rankings arrived, and then I saw some turnarounds from the stragglers thanks to familial pressure. Regularly high performers loved it because winners want to be number one on their teams. Anyone who doesn't, or wants to hide from accountability, should probably stick to support personnel.

OUT OF KEY METRICS

One summer during my teens, I worked at a local mill and had the crappiest job there. Eight hours a day, I lugged and stacked soaking wet, uncut plywood. Wanting to do a good job, I challenged myself to go faster and stack more than the shift before. Once stacked, the wood was sorted and moved onto one of four "green chains" which could be slowed down or sped up depending upon the productivity of the unmotivated men beside them.

One day, tired of waiting for my coworkers to do their jobs, I loaded wood myself, speeding up the chains as often as possible. The other guys, who kept the chains at a constant crawl, noticed me running literal circles around them and were obviously annoyed. They didn't want to go faster. They wanted to slow down because they got paid either way, so why not go slow? It was a union job and these guys didn't care about doing their best. The mentality was *let's work as little as we can and collect the cash.*

It happens in many other fields, too, with tenured employees making the most money regardless of whether they're at the top of their games or not. There are exceptions, but as a rule, if you promote people and give them raises based primarily on length of employment, that system will eventually fail. That's so much of what caused the decrease in American productivity and contributed to the large number of unengaged workers. Wages got so high that they no longer matched up with the jobs, causing companies to outsource to other countries for survival.

Taking a Toll

In the early 1990s, the bidding to build a Southern California toll road, State Route 73 from Costa Mesa to San Juan Capistrano, opened up to private industry. My friend proposed that he could construct the road in less time than government bidders, under the condition that he could keep the tolls collected for the number of weeks he saved by completing the work early. He got the job and several months of tolls. He paid his people well and made a lot of money. This is free enterprise as compared to government-run agencies.

REVIEWS: CHECK, PLEASE

Annual reviews as a measurement of employee performance are passé. Just as managers shouldn't set goals 365 days in advance because that's too far away to have any meaning, they shouldn't wait an entire year to check on progress either. By waiting too long to review numbers, managers will find that most employees are under the bar and don't know how they got there (or they know but were hoping no one else did).

Another purpose of regular performance evaluation is to encourage communication between managers and team members. Beyond giving feedback on performance, managers should also evaluate a team member's skill set in relation to what's needed to execute their role effectively. They should also make suggestions for improvement and remind employees of the goal line—when outstanding performance has been achieved and it's time to celebrate.

As a manager, I consistently checked on my team members' progress. I measured everyone exactly the same way, beginning with daily activity logs early in the relationship, until employees earned the right to move to weekly measurement, then monthly, and finally, quarterly. As a CEO, I received ongoing feedback from my leadership team and together we initiated appropriate changes when performance goals weren't being met. Again, it's work, but it's vital work that a good leader needs to do.

Three keys for scoring performance:

1. **Performance against goals as indicated in their plans.** Feedback on each person's performance as defined by individual and organizational key metrics.

2. **Progress on personal development.** An assessment of a team member's strengths and challenges, noting areas that would benefit from additional training or development.

3. **Behaviors and attitudes.** Suggested modification for better work habits. There are many high performers who negate their performance with bad behaviors and/ or attitudes. Toxic attitudes get more people fired than non-performance. There are three types of people: positive, negative and neutral. Like in electricity, only the positive generates the power.

TO THINE OWN SELF (APPRAISAL) BE TRUE

Although performance evaluations happen routinely throughout the year, it's helpful to have team members complete a written self-evaluation annually. Self-appraisals are another opportunity for valuable communication between managers and team members. Both parties fill out the same evaluation form, and then look for variances. Any difference of opinion warrants a discussion. For example, if an employee thinks he's the most proactive person on the team, and the manager disagrees, together they need to find out why.

This process not only helps employees feel like they're being heard, but it also challenges them to take an honest look at their work habits and behaviors. This should be when team members ask themselves the all-important questions: *What am I not doing that I need to* **start** *doing? What should I* **stop** *doing that's not effective? What am I doing that's effective and that I can increase or* **continue** *doing?*

CHAPTER 6
It's Hard to Manage

Are you Manager Material?

TAKING CHARGE BRINGS CHANGE

I don't think you can manage people any more than you can herd cats, but you can lead the way by effectively facilitating the efforts of a group in a desired direction. Easier said than done. Leaders who can't inspire and train team members to reach their goals will find that managing a department or team is as futile as corralling felines.

Great managers are great coaches. Those in charge have to look and act like leaders—setting expectations, teaching people how to achieve their individual and team goals, then monitoring progress. Successful management skills can be learned and developed through experience. Training and mentoring, however, can't be faked and you can't be a boss situationally.

You have to lead and mirror the company's values 24/7. Frankly, being a manager and role model is exhausting and often unfair. You can make the right decisions practically every time then make one judgment error and you're suddenly a dirtbag.

Managers are expected to:

- arrive first at the office and leave last.

- work nights and weekends, and there's no such thing as clocking out.

- give up control of their personal income and must motivate and incentivize others to get the job done instead.

- be the last ones to get paid, and during tough times, may not get paid at all.

- depend on the performance of others instead of their own, limiting their influence on the outcome. (Many legendary players could control games by scoring at will. However, when they became coaches they discovered few players had their work ethic or talent, and it was hard for them to figure out how to win games relying on others.)

- take responsibility for every mistake or failure because the proverbial buck stops with them.

- accept that recognition goes to team members. Being a good leader means not always taking credit for success.

- endure constant scrutiny by people who are waiting for them to fail, make a mistake, or compromise their values.

THE MANAGER EFFECT

> Coming together is a beginning. Keeping together is
> progress. Working together is success.
> - Henry Ford

The employee-manager relationship is the single most important factor influencing employee engagement. According to Gallup research, an overwhelming 70% of an employee's motivation is influenced by his or her manager. That statistic makes this next finding especially troubling: only 35% of U.S. managers are engaged, while 51% are disengaged, and 14% are actively disengaged.

In view of the troubling state of employee engagement in the U.S. today, it's not surprising that the majority of managers aren't creating environments in which employees feel motivated or even comfortable. A Gallup study of about 7,500 U.S. adults revealed that one in two had left jobs at some point to get away from their managers and improve their quality of life. However, motivated employees are 87% less likely to quit, according to a Corporate Leadership Council study.

The best (the A players) want to be paid well, but more importantly they want to work for A players who care about them and value their opinions. Companies that get performance management right are competitive and successful. However, poor management and unmotivated employees can cost companies in many ways:

- By Gallup's estimates, the managers of the unengaged and actively disengaged cost the U.S. $319-398 billion annually through their unfavorable impact on those they manage.

- Research from the University of California found that motivated employees were 31% more productive, had 37% higher sales, and were three times more creative than unmotivated employees.

- Sales teams led by inspiring leaders are 6% more productive than those that have an average leader and that 6% accounts for an extra $1 billion in annual revenue. (Source: Dell)

- Employees who exercise their strengths on a daily basis are 8% more productive and six times more likely to be engaged. (Source: Gallup)

It's my view that motivation mainly comes from within. Not all managers can motivate all people, but managers can demotivate people by not acting like leaders. For example, making consistently bad decisions, not exhibiting company values, hiring and promoting the wrong people, letting accomplishments go unrecognized and tolerating poor performance are ways leaders can demotivate. Managers have to take a close look at how they're affecting the culture because quality top performers want to work for a company that's consistent and trustworthy across the board

Honey Attracts Money

According to a study by the University of Michigan Business School, the best producing teams used about six times as many positive comments for every negative one. The study also found that the worst performing teams used, on average, three negative comments for every positive one.

Negative feedback diminishes an employee's enthusiasm and commitment, and a manager should seriously consider the risks before doling it out. If managers find themselves uttering more (or even an equal number of) negative comments to positive ones, chances are they're dealing with employees who aren't trained, aren't motivated or aren't in the right jobs.

Basic Boss 101

THE BEST MANAGERS:

- **achieve their numbers quarterly and yearly**. Business is like a game and the score reflects the results of your efforts. You either deliver a win by hitting your goals or you lose, falling short of your budgets and targets.

- **know their cash flow and burn rate at all times.** It may seem obvious, but managers and all company employees should be hyper-aware that without cash flow there will be no company. Another concept they should understand is burn rate, or negative cash flow, an essential measure of how long a business can stay afloat or operate until sales increase or money runs out.

- **do a cash flow forecast.** Businesses have expenditures that are due monthly, quarterly and annually, and failing to prepare for those means scrambling for cash that banks won't always lend you. I regularly have to tell not only managers, but also CEOs, that they're not going to have any money left in six months and they look at me like I'm a martian. They'll insist they've got plenty of money in the bank before I remind them about several big bills coming due. Extremely intelligent people just weren't looking ahead.

- **avoid setting goals that outgrow cash or resources**. Cash flow problems happen during high-growth years, not just when times are tough. Business could be booming, but if companies make a miscalculation, fail to keep up with demand, hire extra employees, or don't collect from clients in a timely manner, a shortage occurs. A shortage creates a negative bank account balance.

- **don't expect what they don't inspect.** Managers must inspect progress regularly, communicate which resources or systems are necessary for team members to meet objectives and be accountable for their team's metrics, as well as their own. Discovering potential problems and correcting them as soon as possible can head off failure.

YOU KNOW WHAT THEY SAY ABOUT THOSE WHO ASSUME

Managers can't assume team members know something, or be the only ones concerned about the company's financial health. For instance, a warehouse manager must be taught that if something doesn't ship by the close of month-end, then based on GAAP, (Generally Accepted Accounting Principles) that revenue can't be recognized and doesn't exist that month. The repercussions could be catastrophic.

Any leader whose warehouse manager makes that mistake is equally responsible and should be held accountable. When team members don't achieve their financial goals, they're not only losing out on bonuses but also risking that the bank may call the company's note. If that happens, no one will have jobs because the business could be history.

MOB MENTALITY LEVELS THE PLAYING FIELD

About 30 years ago, Tom Peters, a global bestselling author and expert on the most effective practices for businesses and their leaders, gave a management seminar. I was one of the 500 in attendance when he asked, "How many of you are in middle management?"

Back then, management was more about shuffling reports from one person to another than producing income directly. Everyone raised their hands. "Then you all better go back to your companies and quit," he warned his dumbstruck audience. Because, if we didn't have numbers after our names (meaning if we weren't personally responsible for generating revenue regularly) we wouldn't have a job in five years. And, of course, his prophecy came true.

Management evolves with the way business is done. In the past, company management was multi-level. For example, every five people had one manager, every group of five managers had a vice president(VP), and every four VPs had a senior VP. Today, organizations are flatter and more collaborative. Instead of a manager for every five people, companies now have diverse, interactive work groups led by technology-proficient team members.

Collaborative development, or mob programming, is when an entire team works on the same project simultaneously, in the same space and at the same computer. Projects get done faster and team members aren't sitting on islands by themselves. For example, instead of 20 code developers, each independently working on a piece of a code, they're divided into four groups of five. One member of each group takes turns managing the keyboard while the other team members give input. Now instead of having to fit 20 pieces together, there's only four pieces, making it numerically easier to accomplish the goal.

Motivating the Masses

WHAT'S THE INCENTIVE?

Besides explaining the company vision, strategies for getting there and milestones that mark progress toward goals, managers must incentivize team members to take ownership of their individual tasks or projects. The way to do that is by making sure employees have some skin in the game. In other words, employees win or lose based on the success of the company, which elicits more commitment from them.

For example: I'm running a warehouse and Jim, who's making $20 an hour, is the guy responsible for putting product into boxes. I say to Jim, "We currently spend $100,000 on boxes, but I'd like you to find less expensive boxes." Pause. "Want to know what's in it for you?" Jim is suddenly all ears. "You'll make 2 cents on every dollar you save the company but if the boxes are cheaper *and* environmentally-friendly, you'll make 4 cents on every dollar saved." Now Jim's totally engaged. On a rudimentary level, that's how you tie someone to costs, company goals and personal incentive.

Without a doubt, employees are more productive and absent less when they're satisfied with their jobs and are fairly compensated. And, though issuing a well-earned bonus is one way to raise morale, there are several other ways that owners frequently overlook.

MONEY ISN'T EVERYTHING TO EVERYBODY

Money can only incentivize so much. We all need money to subsist but it doesn't wake everybody up in the morning. Once people's fundamental needs are met and they can pay their bills and provide for their families, the psychological benefits of greenbacks are arguable. In fact, research shows that financial motivation rarely prompts change in behavior. After all, how motivating would even a six-figure salary be if you're overworked, underappreciated and surrounded by disengaged people and led by a tyrannical leader?

Despite little correlation between salary and job satisfaction levels—even across cultures and geographies—many companies continue to use money as the primary incentive. Then these companies—overloaded with people working solely for the money—experience above-average turnover because whenever such employees are offered a nickel more they jump ship. A business also shouldn't have someone overly motivated by money doing their books—roughly 10% of the companies in our groups experienced theft at the hands of accountants, bookkeepers and controllers.

It's only when managers find the right incentives for their people (keeping in mind different people respond to different motivations) that turnover decreases and employees become more inspired to perform. Employee engagement firm TINYPulse found in its report, *The 7 Key Trends Impacting Today's Workplace*, that only 7% of the 200,000 workers surveyed ranked money as a motivating factor, making it seventh on the list. What really matters to employees is being enthusiastic about going to work instead of dreading it like the majority of the workforce. Today's employees want career development opportunities and training, improved cooperation among workers, a healthy relationship with managers and for their contributions to be recognized and praised far more than they want an increase in pay. Progressive employers who look beyond monetary rewards and accommodate these desires will significantly boost productivity.

The same holds true with millennials and what motivates them. It's not all about the dough. According to Collegefeed, a marketplace that helps college students and graduates find career opportunities, when pursuing employment nearly 80% of millennials look for a culture fit that prioritizes the wellbeing of its workers, followed by career potential and developmental opportunities. The benefits and perks they truly care about are those that offer them greater flexibility, and the ability to lead a better life — even if it means working for less money. They're not afraid to change jobs to find what they want, but once they find it they're particularly loyal.

Currently, 50% of the world's population is under the age of 30, the highest youth population in history. Since millennials comprise an increasing part of the workforce, this trend will only become more significant, having a drastic impact on the identity of company cultures and the new generation of employees. Millennials want different things than their senior coworkers, so managers shouldn't try to incentivize them in the same way.

For example, my fellow CEOs (who are in their sixties) who are trying to entice millennials by holding a contest with a luxury car as the grand prize are going to be disappointed. That won't motivate young professionals. They'd rather live downtown and walk to places or use Uber or Lyft, and many of them don't even own cars. There are speakers and trainers who educate business leaders about millennials and how to relate to, motivate and lead them. However, this isn't really a new issue in business since every generation has to learn to deal with its younger workforce.

Autonomy, or the freedom to manage oneself, is a strong motivator for many top performers, regardless of the generation they were born into. I awarded autonomy to salespeople, for instance, after they earned the right by proving their production over time, and demonstrating a superior work ethic. This incentive is for A players who, when given the tools necessary to do their jobs, can be trusted to keep managers informed and to ask for help when they need it. Managers incentivize these elite employees by allowing them to make their own decisions and then getting out of their way, counseling them only if they get off track.

Sometimes the personal growth aspect as an incentive is also overlooked. For more and more professionals, education and even trips are great incentives. I've had people in finance who wanted to pursue more advanced degrees, so we paid for courses after they achieved their goals, which paid dividends to the business too. Companies that invest in improving, educating and rewarding employees with wider opportunities get the best results.

Lastly, employees want flex time. Researchers at the University of Minnesota and the MIT Sloan School of Management studied a Fortune 500 company to find out if flexible work options have any real, measurable benefits. They discovered that 33% reported having left a job, and 14% said they've considered leaving one because they didn't have access to flexible work options. Those receiving more control over their schedules felt more supported by their bosses, were more likely to say they had enough time to spend with their families, and reported greater job satisfaction, less burnout and lower stress.

I had a long-time HR director, a highly competent and trusted professional who always got the job done. So, when she had her second child, we made arrangements for flex hours and she not only valued the flexibility, but also the respect we afforded her. The ability to telecommute was far more valuable to her than a monetary raise at the time.

Other components of incentive and compensation include: retirement plans, profit sharing and equity or phantom equity programs for top performers. Phantom equity programs give contractual rights to profits, distributions and proceeds from a sale rather than ownership in the company.

GOT GAME?

At age ten, I rocked my paper route. I covered three blocks of about twenty-two houses each and most of them got the newspaper. I made a game of challenging myself to get it done faster and faster without losing any papers to a Calgary snowbank. I measured success by the clock, but also by tips at Christmas.

My next job was harvesting worms from Canadian lawns, which involved soaking the grass then sticking two pieces of metal attached to a car battery into the wet ground. Connecting the battery sent a shock through the ground and made the worms surface. I got paid per box of worms and, of course, made a game of it. I made a lot of fisherman happy when I resold the worms.

Games help make all kinds of jobs (especially repetitive ones) fun instead of drudgery. Gamifying, the term for turning a task or goal into a game, is a modern workplace tool used by savvy managers to create more enjoyment and recognition around progress. Apps that measure progress, motivate users with the chance to win, receive rewards or gain recognition. They also give employees the ability to break jobs into smaller, more manageable tasks, which improves their focus and performance.

At last count, there were over 700 goal-tracking apps available, almost all of them free. They help employees of every level track business and personal goals and habits, and assist managers in measuring an employee's productivity and engagement. Since 70% of business transformation efforts fail due to lack of engagement, a good leader understands the documented success these games offer. Incorporating goals into their digital lives, people keep them front and center and stay motivated. Some apps even allow people to make goals public, fostering accountability and support from friends and family.

GAME ON!

The most successful managers get creative with incentives. One business I work with is a commercial painting company, PacWest Painting. CEO Tony Hady and his management team figured out that their workforce was motivated by games and things other than cash bonuses, so they got innovative. Every time an employee reaches a goal they receive silver stars on their uniforms and after earning five stars they win a prize. When they earn another five stars they get to choose from bigger prizes, and so on. The company has been doing this for three years, growing consistently and retaining key long-term employees.

The Pay-off

PERFORMANCE PAY

The practice of fixed compensation with a guaranteed, yearly salary increase is becoming a business relic, and frankly, I approve. Instead, I believe in goal-driven companies, goal-driven incentive programs and paying at or above market rates to people who perform. To that end, measurement and metrics should be tied to employee compensation plans. In other words, I happily over-reward great performers who meet or exceed their goals, and I pay them more than the unmotivated people beside them. I want to make sure the 20% who are doing most of the work are highly incentivized, the middle-range, or B players, are well-incentivized, while the bottom group gets no additional compensation—not a bit more, none! If goals are set correctly then the best people should make the most money.

I'd rather have fewer people making more money versus a bunch of modestly compensated, underperformers. For instance, if a company in my industry has 150 people, I want to do a better job with 100 people and pay them 50% more. Good leaders want to reward their outstanding people because they know that those employees command more compensation and can go elsewhere to get it. Business is the same as pro sports in that regard.

Here's an example of what I mean by goal-driven compensation and salary based on performance:

A staff accountant who earns $80,000 annually could potentially make up to another 50%, or $40,000 more. This comprises 25% ($20,000) tied to personal goals, individual key metrics and over and above performance, and 25% ($20,000) based on the company/department achieving its key metrics. This system works with employees at the manager level and up.

Key reports, who are VP level and above, should be able to earn 100% of their salary in bonuses tied to their goals. Salespeople should always be paid for personal production and be able to make 100% commission equal to their salaries. The best producers in sales will always prefer a smaller salary and an unlimited commission plan.

I also advocate that hourly workers be able to earn an additional 10% of their wages in bonuses tied to their goals and believe in group incentives to motivate team members. I used to have a management team that got bonuses when they achieved their revenue and profit targets. If the team didn't win, individual members couldn't hit their maximum bonuses. Of course, individuals who habitually missed their predetermined and agreed-upon goals wouldn't have to worry about the team goals because they'd likely be looking for new employment.

Title	Salary	Total Bonus Opportunity	50% of bonus (based on achievement) of individual goals) $31,250	50% of bonus(based on company EBIT** revenue at budget) $31,250	Total Compensation
HR Manager	$125,000	$62,500	$25,000	$34,375	$184,375
Percentage			80%*	110%*	
Notes			3 goals/ attained 80%	Company attained 110% of revenue and EBIT targets	

* In the example above, a manager has three key metrics to achieve and each metric is worth 100%. At 100% the maximum bonus is awarded; below 100%, the negative percentage is deducted. On the positive side, if managers achieve over 100% of their goals, then the extra percentage is tacked onto their salaries, too.

** earnings before interest and taxes (EBIT)

RECEIVE AND YOU SHALL GIVE BACK

Regular Social Security cost-of-living adjustments (COLAs) began in 1975 at 8% when inflation was running high. The raises reached their peak of 14.3% in 1980, but lower inflation during the 1990s led to more modest increases, about 2-3% annually. Not a proponent of customary annual employment raises based on the market, I feel that if companies give COLAS, shouldn't they get some money back when there's deflation? Fair is fair.

BIGGER ROLE, BIGGER BUCKS

The topic of salary caps is always a dicey one. I see countless companies get into trouble handing out automatic raises every year when the reality is they can't keep paying more for the same job because of the fundamental aspects of profitability. Firstly, salaries can't keep increasing indefinitely because profits don't necessarily increase commensurate with the ever-increasing business-related costs. Then there's the Peter Principle, which maintains that everyone eventually rises to their level of incompetence in an organization. Employees reach a point when they're no longer deserving of rewards, having become over-matched by the job demands, or in other words, incompetent. Simply being on the job for years doesn't mean someone is entitled to a raise. Not every long-term employee is ready for advancement, and promoting somebody prematurely leads to problems.

The way I see it, if employees want to make more money then they need to take on bigger roles in the company or up their games with more education and training. The bigger the roles people take on, the more money they deserve. Managers should help team members who hit salary ceilings identify their strengths and weaknesses and explore what they can do to be of more value to the business long-term. Still, it must be employee-driven to be meaningful. One employee may want to learn Microsoft Excel and another hopes to enroll in a finance class. Both are ways to expand their skills, and increase their usefulness to their teams.

There are also countless courses that benefit both employees and companies offered by the American Management Association, which provides professional development and training at local colleges and through online programs. As a business owner, I paid for a variety of courses for employees as long as there were mutually agreed-upon timeframes by which the company would recoup its investment with the incorporation of the new skills on the job. Employees are not only grateful for the increase in compensation opportunities, but also for the education.

Perk Prudence is its Own Reward

Intent on being the opposite of the controlling, authoritarian bosses that I hated, I learned a lesson about overdoing it. After a few mishaps with newly-appointed leaders, I wished I'd been stingier with the frequency and overzealous number of rewards I bestowed. In retrospect, I should have been a tad more patient, weighing in the long-term impacts before pulling out the big guns—the corner offices, prestigious titles, company cars, and higher salaries. Those types of rewards can rarely be rescinded.

In the sports arena, an example of acknowledgement gone awry is illustrated with high school and college athletes. Many young athletes, lavished with too much praise and recognition, are unprepared to deal with their newfound fame. They start believing their own PR, thinking they're all that, then negative behaviors emerge which affect their performance. I've seen promising careers blow up this way. I think that the more you can give bonuses that are meaningful (but not over the top) the better it is for you, your people and the company.

Research corroborates my experience. U.S. companies spend tens of billions of dollars on bonuses and incentives while the debate about the effectiveness of the extravagant rewards continues. Studies suggest extra perks produce only temporary sustainment of desired behaviors and attitudes, but as drivers that yield a lasting improvement or commitment they're ineffective. Once the rewards stop, people relapse to their old ways.

PAY ATTENTION

When team members accomplish tasks or meet goals, management should show appreciation by recognizing them in front of the team or throughout the company. Performers will feel that their contributions are appreciated and are more than likely to become long-term company assets. Conversely, unacknowledged successes create cultures where people feel undervalued and unappreciated.

I always tied an employee's goal to a celebration. Celebrating individual and team milestones emphasizes the premise that when team members work collaboratively, odds of success increase.

I've seen companies recognize top performers and big wins in daily announcements, company town hall meetings and newsletters. You can even take a more personal approach and send *thank you for your performance* gifts to employees' homes. People like to be on winning teams and by sharing goals and regularly recognizing performance, other team members know how their colleagues are doing too.

CHAPTER 7
The Leading Role

An effective leader knows the way, goes the way and shows the way. - John C. Maxwell

Boss Behaviors

THE EARLY LEAD

While it's true that certain people may be inherently predisposed to becoming leaders—just as others may be inherently predisposed to becoming athletes or artists—it's also possible to develop the traits necessary to list "boss" on your resume. More than DNA, leadership is cultivated by upbringing, environment and opportunities that foster someone's abilities to take charge and motivate others. If you want to get scientific about it, research suggests that the factors affecting whether someone can lead successfully are one-third genetics and two-thirds practiced, conditioned behaviors.

Early experiences build the foundations for leadership. That's why employers look for former high school captains of the debate and basketball teams or candidates that held roles with responsibility for others during their formative years. Even certain elementary-school-aged children have an unmistakable engrossing charm (rudimentary charisma perhaps?) and a self-assuredness that's not typical among their peers. Other children are drawn to these young charmers, seeking their approval, imitating their actions and following their lead on the playground. And, by the sixth grade, they have no problem identifying those leaders.

When I was chosen as a crossing guard in elementary school (a great honor among my peers) it was the first time I received recognition as a leader, though I didn't realize that at the time. Even in my teens, despite becoming captain of both the junior high and community hockey teams, and receiving the best hockey player in the school award in the tenth grade, I still lacked the confidence to believe I was good enough. Genuinely surprised by the recognition I'd garnered, I chalked it up to my coaches feeling sorry for me. Even years later after experiencing some success in sales I wondered why I was asked to become a manager.

It's not uncommon for some people to recognize leadership in others before they recognize it in themselves. That was certainly true in my case. A friend of mine from junior high told me decades later that my classmates knew I was destined to become a leader. For me, that realization didn't come until I left a *you're lucky to work here* culture and experienced recognition and appreciation. That's when I finally started to believe that I was actually very good at what I did.

THE GREAT ONES ARE OBVIOUS

If you examine extremely successful people such as legendary hockey giants Gordie Howe and Wayne Gretzky, though separated by thirty-five years, they shared similar traits. Always the hardest-working guys in the room, they both had plans and didn't deviate from them. Each move up the professional ladder was strategic, and they were always looking for ways to improve not only physically, but also mentally.

I never visited the Hockey Hall of Fame even though I lived in Toronto, where it was housed. Unlike the Gretzkys and Messiers of the world, whose career achievements now live on there, I didn't have a hunger to know more about my craft. Like other professional greats, both men had an insatiable thirst to know everything they could about the game they loved, their passion. They were students of hockey and I was just a player.

Even into his forties, Gordie wasn't slowing, he remained a force of nature and demanded the respect of all players. He was still in as-good or better condition than the other players in the league. After retiring at forty-five, he returned to the WHA a couple of years later to play with his sons. Getting back into playing shape again to compete alongside teammates in their twenties was no easy feat, but he did just that before retiring for good at fifty-two. I thought about that as I was starting out as a mentor to young entrepreneurs. Like Gordie, I had to be prepared and be on my game if I wanted to relate to new and future colleagues and guide them effectively.

LEADERS MAKE LOUSY SPECTATORS

1. There are people who make things happen.

2. There are people who watch things happen.

3. There are people who wonder, *what happened?*

I'm in category 1. Where are you?

Although I'm a good team player, I'm an unhappy follower.

Even as a kid I always wanted to be in charge. I wanted to be first and at the center of all activity. I blamed that on my hyperactivity, never equating it with a need to lead. I just knew I didn't want anybody to get in my way no matter the situation.

Looking back at my hockey career, I recognized I became an enforcer not because I was mean, crazy, super tough or enjoyed brawling. Rather, I couldn't stand by and watch things happen to my teammates without taking control of the situation and dealing with it personally. If I had been born one hundred years earlier, I would have been a Sheriff. As it turned out, I was no different in business.

In my thirties, as the president of a company for the first time, I joined a leadership group that conducted member-led business forums, and the leaders rotated each year. I had a great experience during my first year because the forum leader was organized, structured and focused. In my second year though, the forum leader was none of those things and I felt I'd wasted sixty hours of my time.

The fact that none of the other CEOs in the group voiced displeasure tested my continuing self-doubt, but not enough for me to ignore the injustice bubbling up inside me. I spoke up. Sure enough, the other CEOs had felt the same way but kept quiet. Hmmmmmmm. That was a turning point. The next year, I volunteered to lead the forum and had such an extraordinary experience that I took over the role permanently. Ultimately, I couldn't be a bystander to failure, or accept the status quo in the office, or anywhere else.

CHIEF CHECKLIST

> **I never dreamed about success. I worked for it.**
> **—Estée Lauder**

Many leaders are competent, but few qualify as remarkable. So, what separates good from great leaders? For starters, it's virtually impossible to become a great leader without being an exceptional communicator. Leaders may possess a vision, for instance, but without the ability to communicate and execute it, they'll have an impossible time. Another common quality among top leaders in all fields is the hunger to learn, improve and grow no matter how successful they become.

Leaders who want to break away from the pack need to personify these other crucial capabilities.

THE BEST LEADERS I KNOW ARE:

- **inspiring.** Good bosses care about the individuals. Basketball coach John Wooden felt that the way you lived, your character and behaviors inspired people to follow. I once asked retired basketball greats and former UCLA Bruins teammates, Bill Walton and Swen Nater, why they thought that Wooden was such an amazing coach. They both pointed to the example the illustrious coach set on and off the court, encouraging his players to succeed in both basketball and life.

- **innovative.** Innovation is a new way of thinking that challenges old ideas, but innovative leaders don't necessarily have to conceive pioneering ideas. Frequently, they're the ones who recognize innovation and visualize the way to turn it into reality. My friend Eric Leitstein owns OMG Restaurant Group in an industry that's notoriously competitive and grueling. He developed a leadership structure that keeps every team member involved in all business aspects from menus and customer experience, to costs and quality. As a result, he cultivated a family of employees that loves the hospitality industry, performs at a high level and delivers outstanding results.

- **empathetic.** This doesn't mean being a pushover but instead having the capacity to understand the feelings and perspectives of others and relate to them in a way that generates comfort and trust. If leaders can tap into how others think and what matters to them, they'll be able to speak and lead more effectively.

- **good listeners.** As Steven Covey, author of *The 7 Habits of Highly Effective People,* says, "Most people do not listen with the intent to understand; they listen with the intent to reply." Listening provides leaders with different ideas and solutions, and helps them coach people with varying personalities and strengths toward a mutual objective. A leader who listens improves morale and teamwork, thereby increasing a team's engagement and loyalty.

- **risk-takers.** Good leaders take calculated risks. They don't ignore facts when making decisions, but rather gather input from trusted people then carefully consider the more difficult path when coming to a fork in the road. The biggest risks I've taken have led to the greatest rewards. Without risk-taking, leaders remain stagnant and ultimately, become complacent.

- **principled.** Leaders can't compromise their values even during challenging times. My mother used to advise me that whenever I had to make a difficult decision, to do so as if it would be broadcast on the nightly news. That stayed with me. In today's world of instant information, many decisions wind up on Twitter and Facebook, disseminated to millions within minutes of being made. I don't think enough people understand the gravity of this.

- **humble.** Allowing others to take the glory and not needing the limelight are signs of a confident leader. When you're really good at what you do, your reputation precedes you. Wayne Gretzky and Gordie Howe were two of the best hockey players ever, and also two of the most humble people. They gave credit but didn't take it. They had healthy egos but kept them in check.

- **tenacious.** After immediately acknowledging any poor decisions or mistakes, tenacious leaders change course as quickly and efficiently as possible, correcting things while continuing to push forward. When leaders avoid or postpone rectifying mistakes, the problems typically grow like fungi with time.

- **trustworthy**. Without the trust of their employees, leaders can't be effective. Trustworthy leaders admit any misdirection or errors in judgment because trust takes time to earn and can be lost in an instant. When teams trust their leaders, ideas flow more freely, and both productivity and creativity increase. With trusted leaders, employees are more at ease with change.

- **self-controlled.** Coach Wooden felt that maintaining his self-control on the bench during games was important. He figured that his players were more likely to stay under control if he remained composed. Coming from hockey, I needed to tone down my behavior in the business world so I could successfully manage others. The best compliment anyone can pay me after learning about the penalty minutes I racked up for fighting in my pro hockey career, is to say, "But you seem like such a nice, calm guy."

Communication Cues

Interpersonal behavior can make or break a leader. While judging a Toastmasters contest, I learned a technique for getting to know someone in minutes from a young contestant battling his fear of public speaking. The exercise is called "FORD," an acronym for remembering what to ask the other person:

- **F**amily (Tell me about your family)
- **O**ccupation (What's your job now and in the past?)
- **R**ecreation (What do you do for fun?)
- **D**ream (What's your vision for the future?)

PIVOT OR PLUNGE

Change is everywhere, and skillful leaders bear a responsibility to refresh their views, challenge their own assumptions and maintain business relevancy. To accomplish this, they have to recognize the signs of what's coming, based on advancements and occurrences happening today, and know when to pivot, or change course and adapt. For example, if 20 years ago you were offered stock in Google and Amazon or Sears and Kmart, which would you have chosen? In other words, Sears and Kmart didn't pivot.

Executed properly, pivoting can transform unsuccessful or ailing businesses into booming ones. The strongest leaders consistently switch gears when difficulties arise instead of getting side-swiped by loss or failure. Countless startups launch with one business model, but when problems surface, instead of folding, the tenacious leaders pivot to something different. YouTube started off as a video dating website called *Tune in Hook up* that didn't work, so the leaders pivoted to a video-sharing platform. The co-founders listened and realized that their users had a better idea of the company's purpose than they did. YouTube worked, took off and was acquired by Google in 2006 for $1.65 billion in stock. It was a sudden shift in strategy that turned an idea into a billion-dollar company.

Pivoting is not only for startups but also for prospering, veteran companies. Faced with increased consumer demand for healthy eating (which grew by as much as 3,400% over the past 20 years), General Mills pivoted to organic foods, buying up a number of such brands, aiming to reach $1 billion in organic and natural food sales. Granted, General Mills saw a slight decrease in net profits (2013-15) prior to pivoting to organic foods, but even so, was far from bankruptcy. The company employed the three P's: planning, proaction and pivoting at the right time. Those companies that can't adapt are in jeopardy.

Fewer than 12% of the Fortune 500 companies included in 1955 were still on the list in 2017; the other 88% have either gone bankrupt, merged with (or were acquired by) other firms, or still exist but have fallen off the list. *Why?* Instead of constantly innovating, those leaders lost touch with technology, industry transformations and customer demands. The late Red Scott, former CEO of Intermark Inc. (a Fortune 500 company) and a valued mentor, warned me years ago it's the unknown factor coming down the road that'll destroy your business.

LEADERS DO TIME

The truth is not everybody can lead. Most people aren't cut out for it or don't want the pressure of being responsible for others or for making decisions… or mistakes. They'd rather follow than lead, and that's okay. There are also those misguided souls who want to be in charge without doing the work to earn their stripes, though overnight leadership successes rarely happen.

These legendary head coaches paid their dues first, studying and practicing their crafts before enjoying any success:

- **John Wooden** spent eleven years as a high school coach and teacher before becoming head coach at UCLA and winning 10 NCAA national championships within twelve years.

- **Bear Bryant** was an assistant college coach for about nine years before winning six national and thirteen conference championships as head coach of the University of Alabama football team, holding the record for most wins in collegiate football history.

- **Scotty Bowman** coached junior hockey for eleven years before coaching in the NHL and becoming the only head coach to win a record nine Stanley Cups with three different teams.

COACHABILITY: A LEADER'S KRYPTONITE

Being coachable doesn't just apply to athletes. It's equally as vital for business leaders or anyone who wants to grow, learn, excel or change. If someone's not coachable, then that person must believe they're always right, which means they're uninterested or unwilling to learn new things, expand their views or self-reflect, and may be unable to find value in the feedback of others. I can relate. In hockey, my major league and junior league amateur coaches, utilized fear as their primary coaching technique. This meant that, as a hard-headed young man, I took instruction as criticism and a weakness on my part, which meant I wasn't coachable in this environment.

My first truly effective leader was my father because he was such a good teacher. I needed somebody who'd go out on the ice with me and demonstrate how to do something in a simple, straightforward fashion instead of just yelling at me to shoot the puck. In my twenties, having played juniors and pro for several years, my father was the first one to spot that I was shooting off the wrong foot. He instructed me to shift my weight to the other foot and I saw better results immediately.

When working with CEOs and other top-ranking leaders, especially young ones, the first thing I try to determine is if they're coachable because if they're not, they can't improve. After years of experience, I've discovered the people who are most adamant about being coachable usually aren't. They'll insist they want to be coached, or say someone else suggested it, then proceed to do most of the talking, instead of listening to what I advise. If they don't listen, they can't hear what they need to learn and can't be coached, so those leaders often bounce from coach to coach without accomplishing anything.

Originally, I saw the hard cases as challenges and refused to give up on them, but over time I realized that they rarely changed. The first two coaching clients I took on were both young, successful entrepreneurs eager for me to work with them, yet uncoachable. They'd ask for advice and without fail—ignore it. Repeatedly. Don't get me wrong. I never want to work with people who take every proposal or idea I have without question. However, when given constructive criticism, they need to receive it and make a concerted effort to alter their behaviors.

One of the CEOs chronically showed up late for our meetings and didn't do the homework I assigned. I typically give coaching clients a book, such as *The One Minute Manager* by Kenneth Blanchard Ph.D. and Spencer Johnson M.D., then request a one-page report on what they learn simply to see if they care enough to complete it. CEO number-two was on time but couldn't take direction no matter what it was or how it was delivered. I can't fix that. I'm not a psychologist.

After hanging in there for a year, I fired myself because they were wasting my time and theirs. Fast-forward ten years to a call I received from another advisor considering taking on CEO number-two as a client. Over the course of a decade, both CEOs went through 13 coaches and were still behaving the same. What's more, one of them could have sold his company for millions but held out for double the offer and went bankrupt within months of our last meeting. The other person's company, smaller than before, continued to limp along but never achieved its full potential because he wasn't coachable.

Dollars and Sense

A business owner whose company was experiencing 90% new hire turnover came to me for help. He measured success by his annual topline revenue even though his bottom line suffered due to the chronic turnover. Mistakenly, he believed that as long as he hit a particular number in revenue he was succeeding. But it's not how much you make, it's your net income (or total earnings minus the costs of doing business, taxes and other deductions) that determines whether or not a company is thriving. Add to that the cost of mis-hires and that owner made little forward progress. Knowing he was incapable of changing, or being coached, I didn't work with him.

A NEW VIEW

Teams bring comfort and safety, however, once atop the corporate ladder, leaders have to insulate somewhat from theirs. Newly promoted leaders have to readjust their view of things, sometimes literally—if a new office comes with the new title—and figuratively in order to see things consistently without prejudice. That's especially challenging when they've been working with people so long they consider them friends. That shift in authority is seldom easy.

Whether players go into coaching or employees are promoted to leaders, the transition can be rocky. It takes resolve for leaders to keep a respectable distance yet still be a part of the team. To maintain my objectivity, I always kept a slight distance between me and my team.

Leaders need team members to respect them and sticking to the safe-distance rule is one way to ensure they do. This concept is particularly hard for young leaders because many of them want to be liked. Still, odds are good they can be both liked and respected even if they don't become every employee's best friend.

The Evolution of a True Leader

KNOW THYSELF, CHANGE THYSELF

Self-actualized people know who they are and those around them concur. People who aren't self-aware have some opinion of themselves that conflicts entirely with the real world and poses many challenges to leading. Leaders (or anyone for that matter) who aren't self-aware can't evolve. How can you understand and inspire others if you don't know yourself or have a particular blind spot that you can't recognize? I once had a manager who was straight from the Attila the Hun school of management. His demeanor and style let you know that you were replaceable at any time. As smart as he was and as successful as he still managed to be, I know he could have achieved much more if he'd been willing or able to see a need for change.

There's tremendous fallout from high-level professionals who are either convinced that they can't—or won't—change their ways. What happens, for example, if they're clueless that their presentations are boring or weak and aren't connecting with their team members? Or, what if they don't realize that they come across as combative, or chronically negative, or consistently set unrealistic team goals? The result is damaged company culture that significantly impacts employee morale and productivity, and therefore, the future of their businesses.

I've seen leaders and CEOs change with coaching and hard work, but in order to change—especially when it's a long-time unwanted behavior or habit—there has to be a good reason to. (This includes a traumatic life event such as a termination, bankruptcy, divorce, the death of a loved one or serious health issues.) Otherwise, delusional self-confidence causes the real hard cases to resist change, and they simply move their distorted self-image to the next opportunity leaving destruction in their wake.

Ironically, it was at the company with a challenging culture that I mentioned in chapter 3, where I first took the eye-opening DISC assessment which is considered the gold standard of psychological assessments and is used in government, educational institutions and businesses. The basic concept is that knowing your personality type helps you ascertain your strengths and interact more effectively with others. I'm not even sure why the CEO signed off on such a test, except perhaps to compile data that would help make the company more attractive for eventual sale.

The person analyzing the results told me I'd earned the highest score in competitiveness he'd ever seen. Figuring a killer instinct to crush competitors and a take-no-prisoners attitude in sales were undoubtedly desirable traits, I was pleased with my results. I figured wrong. My competitive level was off the charts according to the expert—and my colleagues, too, as they confirmed in a 360° review. A healthy competitiveness is necessary, but mine was blatantly imbalanced.

The reason I managed to adapt and still win more than I lost in that win-at-all-cost environment, was likely because of the fighting mentality leftover from my hockey days. I resorted to my inner enforcer. In essence, I walked into a job that was made for me. Of course, no one ever questioned my aggressiveness in sports, but the truth is had I been able to dial it back I would have accumulated half the penalty minutes, played twice as much, and still been plenty tough. In retrospect, enforcers may have been needed on every team, but goal scorers got paid the big bucks. Lesson learned… twice.

At my next job, which had a different culture, I relearned what was appropriate in terms of how I asked for things, and cultivated better interpersonal skills. Because of the personality assessments and coworker feedback, I modified my behavior, which positively influenced my career—but then again, I *wanted* to improve. I recognized early on that I'd have a better chance of achieving my aspirations if I learned how to work harmoniously with others instead of trampling over them.

I also learned that this type of psychological testing isn't a one-time process. For maximum effect, I recommend leaders do assessments, in conjunction with employees doing a 360° version, every three to five years or within six months of changing roles, and then compare them. Nowadays, I think that the DISC personality test is the most widely-used, and I've employed it many times throughout the years. I took the same profile test three years later at my new job, where I helped shape the culture, and scored exactly where I should be.

Besides utilizing psychological testing, leaders or anyone committed to changing should write an action plan with achievable, daily mini-accomplishments and longer-term goals. Then they should confide in someone they trust who can coach and help them achieve their objectives. We should all confront our limitations head-on if we want to grow.

FACING FEARS: ALWAYS A WIN

At seventeen, while playing in a Canadian Major Junior Hockey League against mostly men in their twenties, my coach, in a rare, genteel moment, asked me if I was scared. My biggest fear was getting beat up in front of my teammates, the other team and the crowd, and losing my identity and reputation as a menacing defender. I answered truthfully: *Hell, yes*.

That's when he revealed to me something I'd never considered, that my opponents were more scared than I was. After all, they were bigger and older with established reputations. I was expected to lose, he said, but if I win… WOW! And if it ended in a draw (as often happens), then no harm. The important thing to understand was that facing fear is never as bad as running from it because then I was sure to lose. That night, I fought two of the toughest guys in hockey at the time and kept up with them. That's when I understood that mental toughness is as important as physical toughness.

I applied my coach's lesson in business to overcome my habits of avoidance and procrastination when facing difficult tasks. In a training meeting on time management years later, I learned that doing the thing I feared most first each day made the rest of the day easy and relieved my stress. I'm a recovering procrastinator but I continually work at it, overcoming it most days now.

BREAKING BAD HABITS

The higher the level of executive responsibility, the more challenging it can be to change bad habits. Recognizing them may be the first step, however, it's the ability to adjust those behaviors before the effects prove damaging, that separate the truly insightful leaders from the complacent ones. That's why some companies hire external coaches or advisors—such as someone from the board of directors, an advisory member or another type of consultant—to pinpoint bad leadership habits and work with leaders toward change. An executive coach, CFO or any other C-level executive who isn't fearful of chastisement for holding the boss accountable can also help obtain accurate feedback from peers and direct reports. In any event, these undesirable habits and/or attributes don't go away magically. They have to be worked on.

An excellent book on this subject is, *What Got You Here Won't Get You There* by Marshall Goldsmith. In his book, Goldsmith identifies behaviors that keep leaders from becoming their best. He proposes that behavioral problems, not technical skills or personality flaws, are what trip up many leaders.

Hired by boards of Fortune 500 companies to work with CEOs who may be struggling, Goldsmith has clients evaluate themselves and specify their unfavorable behaviors. Next, he instructs them to ask the three people they work with most frequently—often a CEO will choose the CFO, and the VPs of sales and marketing—to point out and discuss these particular behaviors whenever they see them arise. I apply this process to all employees wanting to make changes, including myself.

Some leadership habits on Goldsmith's list are subtler than others and on the surface don't appear to be harmful, however, in reality, they're serious impediments to effective leadership. I worked on overcoming the first two issues below but have included some others as well:

1. **Winning Too Much: The need to win at all costs and in all situations** (when it matters and even when it doesn't). This was a tough one for me because I had to be aware of the problem before I could fix it, then constantly stay on top of it. It wasn't until my forties that I began managing this issue properly. My mindset had always been that I had to win every discussion, negotiation or business agreement. I felt that simply changing my mind was comparable to losing, so once I had an opinion I had to live or die by it. Unfortunately,

it also meant that I wasn't hearing or open to other perspectives or ideas, and that makes you do dumb things. It was a chronic problem that reared its ugly head not only during business, but also in mundane daily activities. Eventually I learned that being flexible yields better results.

2. **Adding Too Much Value: The overwhelming desire to add our two cents to every discussion.** Delegating, or more specifically, letting people come up with ideas and succeed or fail on their own was tough for me. Instead, I automatically took over, especially when I knew that my experience would lead to the best results. It's been a learning process, working harder than I had to before, recognizing that if I wanted my people to grow then I had to allow them to handle things without my intervention.

In my first job as a senior executive, the chairman (a very principled guy and a valued mentor) espoused the value of checking your ego, surrounding yourself with great people and then allowing them to do their jobs. I took his advice and no longer feel the need to micromanage. Now, when people approach me with problems, I allow them first to come up with their own solutions by asking, *What do you think you should do?* Then if necessary, I guide them in the correct direction. By making this adjustment I also learned that when team members take ownership of the problems and solutions, they become insanely productive.

Other bad habits that Goldsmith helps CEOs combat, include:

- **Refusing to express regret.** The inability to take responsibility for our actions, admit when we're wrong or recognize how our actions affect others.

- **Failing to give proper recognition.** The inability to praise and reward.

- **Telling the world how smart we are.** The need to show people we're smarter than they think we are.

- **Making destructive comments.** The needless sarcasm and cutting remarks we think make us sound sharp and witty.

- **Withholding information. The refusal to share information in order to maintain an advantage over others.**

- **Playing favorites.** Failing to see when we're treating someone unfairly.

LEARN TO LEAD

> Leaders aren't born, they are made. And they are made just like anything else, through hard work. - Vince Lombardi

As a young athlete, although I considered my abilities inferior to most, I worked hard and practiced relentlessly, doing everything possible to expand my capabilities and get to the

Major Leagues—and I did as a rookie. Even so, having finally arrived at what I believed to be the final destination, I stopped doing the hard work that got me there in the first place and that I needed to keep doing in order to stay.

Other players who weren't as big, as fast or necessarily more skilled than me played pro hockey for more than twice as long as I did because they never quit working at their crafts. As soon as I'd made the pros and the big bucks, however, I backed off on the intensity of my training. When I should have been focusing on getting even better over the off-season, I opted for travel and a bit too much fun instead. Determined not to let that happen in business, I knew I had to keep improving to stay on top.

Although I didn't always have what it took to be the best of the best, and even struggled with low self-esteem in business, I thankfully discovered that being a leader had little to do with aptitude or talent. Leadership is about skills, attitudes and behaviors that for the most part can be emulated and learned. In other words, someone could be innately smarter than me or have more education than me, but I could apply myself and learn to be just as good—or even better. I'm living proof that most leadership skills can be acquired.

You can learn to:

- **communicate better.** The ability to communicate with all kinds of people in a variety of situations is probably the most important characteristic of an effective leader. The good news is that anyone can develop better communication skills through simple learning tools and practice.

- **be charismatic.** To many people's surprise, charisma can be honed. You can develop it by observing others who come by it naturally and mimicking their habits and behaviors. That's how I did it. Now, whenever I coach someone who feels deficient in this area (a common theme among budding CEOs) I ask them to describe three people that they consider charismatic and then we practice the traits they admire.

- **listen better.** Being a good listener is also part of being a good communicator. Listening is a skill that can be acquired and developed with practice. One technique, active listening, involves focusing fully on the speaker while displaying verbal and non-verbal signs of listening.

- **show empathy.** Empathy, the ability to understand the feelings of others, is a necessary leadership skill that can be mirrored, practiced and improved.

- **improve financial knowledge**. Effective financial management is vital for business survival and growth. Starting out, I had to learn about cash flow, balance sheets, KPIs and other business basics. All leaders have a responsibility to understand the fiscal side of their companies if they want to lead effectively. Mentors are excellent sources for this type of information.

- **change your image.** On my first day of work in business, I pulled up in an orange and brown travel van sporting a full mullet and Fu Manchu moustache.

No longer a flashy professional athlete, I was in a business-to-business sales position, which called for conservative attire, such as blue suits, red ties and white starched shirts. I overheard a few snickers for sure that first morning, so a haircut, shave and midsize car soon followed.

You cannot learn:

- **work ethic or perseverance.** You either have it or you don't.

- **to become someone you're not.** For example, trying to adapt a leadership style that doesn't feel natural or be someone other than yourself, comes across as disingenuous and that's the fastest way for a leader to lose trust.

- **creativity.** Specific behaviors and strategies related to the creative process can be demonstrated, but not taught.

- **integrity.** Most experts agree that by the time we hit our twenties, the extent of our integrity has been mostly formed. You can't teach someone who's fundamentally dishonest to be completely honest and you can't teach good character to someone with life-long negative vices. You can only make people aware of the consequences of their actions and hope they improve over time.

- **intuition.** Also known as a gut feeling, intuition is the capacity to reason and arrive at a decision without solid proof. It's a natural ability that can only be honed.

MONKEY SEE, MONKEY DO BETTER

Hanging out with better people makes you less uncertain about the unknown. When I went into sales, I studied the top three salespeople in the company. The number-one salesperson was an affable guy with great people skills. Salesperson number-two's strong suit was his amazing work ethic, but people in operations hated him because of his demanding and entitled attitude. As a result, sometimes his orders would mysteriously get *lost*. The number-three guy didn't work as hard as number-two but kept his numbers up and operations loved him. And, just like that, by watching others I added to my arsenal of tools in my new career:

1. Develop customer relationships.
2. Work hard.
3. Make friends with the operations team.

Taking the Lead, Making Choices

GROWING A COMPANY

People want to be a part of an award-winning, growth-oriented company because it's exciting and there's potential to excel and grow along with it. If your company doesn't grow, someone else's will, and your good employees will work there. So, why do some CEOs win and expand companies while others just stay the same or fail? Is it luck? Talent? Opportunity? Intelligence? Perhaps all of these to some extent?

Upon entering the business world, I felt as if I had none of those things but, even so, I still achieved success by focusing and having a plan. With a plan, you can join just about any team and turn it around short-term, but short-term turnaround doesn't get you long-term results. Long-term survival requires more.

Sage Executive Group forum members collectively studied the growth of their companies over three years to find out what attributes separated high growth from mediocre growth. The most prevalent factors behind business growth were company owners' drive to outgrow competitors and their willingness to create opportunities for their employees. Additionally, high-growth companies had aggressive plans that tied all employees to them, hired as many A players as possible to drive the plans, cultivated leaders who created cultures that promote and reward both productivity and innovation, outworked the competition, constantly coached and developed their people, and resisted complacency.

Prior to March 2020 and the COVID-19 crisis, we were in an economy for ten years where the rising tide was floating all boats, so some luck may have been involved for many companies. However, deciding how to grow a business must be driven by intention, not luck. Determining how to pivot your business will be important going forward. I've known that hard work and fortitude beat talent any day, so the harder I worked the luckier I got. Besides, growing companies during good times isn't a measure of success. Growing a company during difficult economic times is the real test of a thriving business, requiring skill and forethought. In tough economies, I've seen large public companies that were running fat immediately cut costs, services and people, and small companies with limited resources that had been riding the wave of good conditions go under. It's mid-market companies with good cash reserves and a flexible operating plan that fare best during these challenging times.

Still, no matter what the economy does, businesses that don't experience a minimum of 6% growth annually while costs (such as healthcare, payroll, real estate, technology, minimum wage and more) continually rise, eventually go away. For example, let's say you're a $100-million company and you make a 10% income, which is $10 million. If you don't increase your top *and* bottom line each year as annual expenses increase, the next year you'll make $9 million. If you don't grow the following year, you'll make $8 million, and so on. So, if you open your doors every year with a plan just to make the same profit as last year, you still better increase sales each year. The exceptions to these standards are situations like the global financial crisis or a global pandemic where we don't know when the rebound will turn businesses back in a positive direction.

Another current issue facing many great companies who are on a trajectory to grow, is the depletion of good employees who are courted by crappy companies. Without strong cultures and/or long-term plans, struggling companies regularly *buy* their people and resources from flourishing ones. That brain-drain takes its toll, and education is the only deterrent. Great company cultures must include teaching employees about businesses that offer too-good-to-be-true money before those unstable companies lure them away.

Employees need to look at job changes like stock purchases and check into a company's financials first. Failing businesses do incredibly stupid things to stay afloat, including paying people exorbitant prices that they can't sustain. For example, someone who's making $100,000 may be offered $150,000 when the company could have easily hired the person for $110,000. That creates a buying frenzy that's not sustainable. Companies have to make money, and in most cases, can't afford to pay people up to 50% more just because it's a hot employee's market. They can only afford to pay what their budgets allow and will most likely fail as soon as there's a downturn.

To me it's a no-brainer. If the company isn't experiencing growth, then it needs to do something different. I target 10% growth a year, but that's not only top line growth, it includes net income growth. Company leadership should set the tone and target regarding growth. If the leader thinks 10% is good, then everyone else will, too.

FOLLOW THE LEADER… OR NOT

Evidence suggests that leaders who learn from their own, and others' mistakes are more successful. I think I learned more from the leaders I didn't admire than those I did. I recall many times when I'd watch the latest *flavour-of-the-month* leader make decisions and think, I wouldn't do *that*. Still, the reality is that we're in a capitalist society and measured by the revenue and profit we produce, so leaders feel the unrelenting pressure of knowing that they're only as good as their last year. That pressure sometimes pushes leaders to make questionable decisions.

During my time in both small private companies and big public ones, I saw the most egregious sins committed just to achieve short-term quarterly earnings. One company I worked for doubled the employee healthcare premium mid-year because of a costly business blunder. Instead of forfeiting some earnings, the leaders stuck it to the employees. I could never do that to my people.

In past years, there's been a trend for companies to self-insure their medical benefits to save on premiums—a great concept unless you have a bad year for surgeries and transplants. There's insurance coverage that can mitigate this issue, but one company I worked for decided to forgo paying the premium and the employees took the hit. If I had been the leader of that company I would have sucked it up. The exorbitant consequences to the company due to the lost trust were unrecoverable. Instead of it costing the company a few million dollars had it eaten the loss short-term, it probably cost tens of millions in future revenues.

Quarterly earnings can't be ignored but should never be sought at the expense of losing good people and long-term desired outcomes. I've learned in business and in life that you do the right thing, which often isn't the easiest or expedient thing. In business, always serve your company, customers and employees. All three must be served equally for a process, idea or business to survive in the long run. When companies put people over profit, they'll actually make more profit.

VERY PUBLIC PROBLEMS

Even geniuses can go bankrupt when their only priorities are keeping Wall Street and shareholders happy with the biggest, short-term payoffs. Public company leaders profess that they have this huge responsibility to both their investors *and* employees, and truly care; however, they consistently opt for higher quarterly earnings—often ignoring business fundamentals, and gambling with long-term company stability.

Many public company boards and senior management get paid based on quarterly and annual results, receiving more stock based on stock price increases. Unfortunately, those increases don't necessarily reflect the company's financial or management stability or even that the company does the right things. Since everything is driven by quarterly and yearly cycles, there's no consideration that in five or ten years, decisions made today can damage (or even obliterate) the company's future. It bears repeating: Leaders can't ignore business fundamentals.

There must be both growth and earnings for a business to thrive. GE, once the darling of Wall Street, downsized by 50% because they decided that growing quarterly damaged the company (which lost all its value). In hindsight, leadership realized that they needed to focus equally on earnings. If one has to be jeopardized, growth should go, not earnings. Every time a company grows above a certain percentage, earnings decrease.

In the private sector, company owners don't have to mortgage their companies or convince 100 million shareholders that their decisions make sense because they hold the purse strings. At any time, they can decide to have lower earnings short-term and instead grow and invest more in people and ideas that pay off long-term.

Blood-Red Warning Signs

In recent history a Silicon Valley superstar (and the youngest self-made female billionaire) grew a startup—based on new blood test technology—into a $9-billion firm. This person secured an impressive board of advisors and investors, before an investigation into the accuracy of the product's results by the Wall Street Journal prompted a federal investigation. Subsequently, a disgraced CEO was charged with massive fraud by the Securities and Exchange Commission for misleading not only employees but also investors, who sunk almost a billion dollars into the tainted and now-failed business. The investors blindly ignored basic business fundamentals.

LEADERSHIP ISN'T FOR SISSIES

Some ill-advised people romanticize the role of CEO, believing the job is all prestige and no work. This couldn't be further from the truth. CEOs give up their most valuable commodity when they take on the job: personal time. (Not to mention many hours of sleep!) I remember lying awake through the wee hours of countless nights worrying about payroll, company lawsuits, seemingly insurmountable customer issues, a bomb scare and worst of all the death of employees. These things weighed heavily on me and many times I longed for the days when I was solely an employee instead of a boss.

Fear of failure is a primary motivator for many CEOs, and probably the best prevention for complacency. In sports and business, my biggest fear was failing—myself, my family, my teammates, people I employed, and even their families who all relied on me. Analysis paralysis, over-thinking a situation to the point where a decision or action is never taken, is a byproduct of the fear of failure. If you allow fear to become paralyzing, you lose. However, if you face your fears and fail, you learn.

That's not to say that anyone wants to fail—especially leaders whose serious mistakes don't only result in lost revenue. Bad or reckless business decisions sometimes cost companies intellectual capital, which it can't get back. Intellectual capital is knowledge or skills that have monetary value. For example, the way a company develops or produces its goods or services is valuable to a competitor. Critical errors in judgment by leadership can also result in the loss of emotional capital (a company's reputation or brand value), which motivates people to keep buying particular products and services.

Sizing Up Leadership Styles
FIND YOUR WAY

I'm a composite of every coach and leader I have ever worked with. I have experienced opposite ends of the spectrum from working with true role models to psychological manipulators. In both hockey and business, I had many old-school leaders who motivated through fear, and reward and punishment to induce a desired behavior. Losing my ranking or job hung over my head like a guillotine blade under their leadership.

Sometimes, fear works. The coaches who haven't yet made the transition from college coaching to the pros, for instance, can get away with fear tactics and a dictator-like leadership style and still enjoy success. Those coaches are well-paid and receive a surplus of new players every year—they might get one hundred players for sixty spots. Meanwhile, amateur athletes aren't compensated and are unable to go elsewhere without huge repercussions. The pros are a different story. Players make more money than their coaches and have more options, including moving to another team. Pro coaches really need to master a more comprehensive leadership style, or combination of styles, or they won't last long.

The command and control leadership style used to be the norm. This approach worked well for driving productivity and efficiency, but today in a quick-changing world of technology, it's become detrimental to employee engagement and innovation. Hierarchical control is outgrowing its usefulness. Instead, new types of leadership that empower all people within an organization to take on greater responsibility and create a collaborative community of shared purpose have moved to the forefront.

Even so, there's no one-size-fits-all leadership style, which means there's more than one way to lead successfully. You need to be able to adapt your approach to fit the position and situation, and complement your core characteristics, personality and decision-making principles. Or, choose the best style of each leader that you admire and see if you can pull it off or modify it to better suit you.

The problem in many cultures is that oftentimes, there's only one great role model and everyone hopelessly tries to mimic his or her style. In family businesses, for instance, it's not unusual for sons and daughters who take over to emulate their parents' style, which doesn't always work. They need to develop their own style, keeping in mind that straying too far from how they usually act and interact with others will come off as insincere. Being true to yourself is the most important thing, and I remembered that in every stage of my career.

Once you choose your style or styles, begin building on and practicing skills to become that type of leader. Just like other newly-acquired skills, you have to practice leadership, and learn it by doing. Gaining a better understanding of what approach feels most authentic, you'll be able to leverage your skills for consistent success.

After enduring bosses who motivated with fear, I always defaulted to positive motivation rather than an authoritarian manner once I became a leader. The old *command and control* leadership that I hated (yet endured from childhood through to my early business career) plagued me for years after, no doubt spurring my problem with authority. On the positive side, being told to do things that I felt didn't make sense, were extreme or downright wrong, contributed to me coming up with a better way. I determined I was going to demand excellence but always let my people know that they were important to me. After all, a CEO's biggest assets are his managers and salespeople.

My leadership approach came from these three, entirely different styles.

1. **Authoritarian (also called *Autocratic* or *Command and Control*).** The inverse of democratic leadership, authoritarian leadership generally involves the exercise of power by the person at the top without input from the team. Employees are neither considered nor consulted prior to a shift in direction, and are expected to adhere to all decisions. It's an old-school method that can work in some companies with few employees.

2. **Democratic (or Participative).** Democratic leaders work closely with their team, focusing on building rapport by inviting input and ideas from all team members. He or she still has the final word, but recognizes that the team may offer beneficial skills and views. It's a good style so long as decisions are made and stuck with. If it becomes too democratic, decisions don't get made and leaders can lose control.

3. **Laissez-Faire**. This is the least intrusive form of leadership. The French term *laissez-faire* translates to *let them do*, and leaders who embrace this style afford most authority to their employees, empowering and trusting them with autonomy. It's an effective style as long as you start with the right people and there's a well-written plan with clearly understood goals and values. Otherwise, it can limit the leader's development, and critical company growth opportunities may be overlooked. Therefore, it's important that this style be kept in check.

Other popular leadership styles include:

- **Servant.** This style, which has experienced a resurgence in attention recently, turns the power pyramid upside down. The leader distributes power among the team and exists to serve the people while delivering great results to shareholders. The servant leader puts the needs of others first, helping them develop and perform as highly as possible to advance. When leaders shift their mindsets and serve first, they inspire purpose and ingenuity that results in more engaged and fulfilled employees.

- **Transformational.** These leaders possess a single-minded need to focus on streamlining or modifying things that no longer work, and specialize in changing the system. They facilitate in setting the vision for the company and guide their people to success by dividing them into integral groups that work well together.

- **Transactional (or Managerial).** Whereas transformational leaders work to change the system, transactional leaders work within the system, minimizing variation and using an archaic system of rewards for performance and punishment for bad results to motivate. Sports teams still depend on transactional leadership. Players aren't inspired to be innovative—instead, they're expected to follow team rules and meet performance expectations, despite possible injury and/or pain.

HOOKED ON HOWE'S LEADERSHIP

Not only a highly-skilled player, Gordie Howe was also a physical player. My father, having played against the formidable number nine many times, warned me to always be cognizant of where Gordie was on the ice because he'd hurt anyone who messed with his teammates. Sure enough, early in one game against Gordie's team, the WHA's Houston Aeros, I found myself in an altercation with a few of his teammates, including his sons Marty and Mark. It was over quickly, and that was the end of it... or so I thought.

Later in the game, I remember skating back up the ice after a routine play and the next thing I knew I was lying on my back with blood in my eye. From behind, Gordie had hooked me in the face with his stick and managed to do it when the refs weren't looking.

I'll never forget weighing my options as I slowly resumed a vertical position. At twenty-one, and as one of the league's enforcers, I was a pretty tough kid in peak shape. Gordie was in his mid-forties, but of course, also in great condition. If I started an altercation with this guy, I thought, one of two things is going to happen:

1. I'll be accused of beating up an old man.

2. More likely, an old man is going to beat me up in front of a packed arena. In the end, I just smiled, and he smiled as we skated back to our respective benches.

To me that's leadership—when you're willing to challenge a pumped-up kid less than half your age. A man of few words, Gordie led through his actions and always backed up his teammates—whether or not they were relatives of his. Especially in business, I'm a firm believer that you should never ask someone to do something that you aren't willing to do yourself. Leaders have to roll up their sleeves and get dirty whenever necessary. Although Gordie was, well… Gordie, he still took care of business. Even when he didn't need to push as hard as the other guys to prove himself, he always outworked and gave more than anyone else. I respect that type of leader.

Out of Style

Greg Lucier had no biotech industry experience whatsoever when he joined Life Technologies, a $500 million company. Coming from General Electric, where he'd run the $5 billion medical device division during the Jack Welch era, Greg quickly realized what he'd been taught was not as effective at Life Technologies. He needed to switch up his leadership style (read: not be such a hard-ass) in order to adapt to his new environment.

A proven leader and avid learner, Greg adopted more of a servant leadership philosophy, allowing him to attract better people and empower them to lead. Greg's self-awareness while at the helm of Life Technologies helped take the business to billions in revenue and facilitate a hugely rewarding exit for its shareholders (nearly $16 billion) which remains one of the largest deals in biotech history.

GREAT LEADERS BREED GREAT LEADERS

> I've learned that you shouldn't go through life with a catcher's mitt on both hands; you need to be able to throw something back.
> – Maya Angelou

Powerful leaders are catalysts for leadership because they bring out the full potential in others. CEOs must cultivate remarkable leaders, or their companies will cease growing. They need to attack the economy and the business world from the ground up. At a granular level, they create great companies that create cultures of great people who create a great economy which funds everything else—because it's never going to get done in Washington D.C.

The best organizations develop leaders by connecting them with other emerging leaders and providing continuing opportunities for the exchange of experience, knowledge and innovation. If you look at any successful company in the United States, many other companies emerge from it. Distinguished companies, such as Microsoft, IBM, Pepsi, and General Motors, all have excellent leader-breeding cultures.

Many of today's best leaders were mentored and encouraged by other outstanding leaders:

- Kevin Systrom and Mike Krieger of Instagram turned to Adam D'Angelo, a former chief technology officer at Facebook and cofounder of Quora

- Richard Branson, founder of Virgin Group credited Sir Freddie Laker, founder of Laker Airways, for inspiration and guidance

- both Larry Page of Google and Mark Zuckerberg, co-founder and CEO of Facebook, counted Apple founder Steve Jobs as a mentor

And the list goes on and on.

My first boss was the gold standard of leaders. Smart, charismatic and self-assured, he recognized talent and developed his people into amazing teams by caring deeply about them, but also by being tough when warranted. Fiercely competitive, he loved to win but hated to lose even more. He was a patient teacher, made work a fun place where you wanted to go, displayed loyalty to his team—and received it in return.

Although I worked for him thirty-five years ago, I still fondly recall when my father came for a visit and my boss took us both to lunch. He spent most of the meal telling my father how good I was at my job and why he enjoyed working with me. Out of the eight salespeople I worked with under his leadership, five went on to become company presidents. If you asked them who they learned from, they'd unanimously give him most of the credit.

Lesser leaders may fear that if their employees become effective leaders they may be replaced by them—and sadly, don't see the success of their people as contributions to their own success. Great leaders don't hinder their team members' progress, they propel it. Without new leaders coming up through the ranks who are trained and challenged by their leaders to work autonomously, they're just other employees who need daily direction and micromanagement, and companies will suffer.

CHAPTER 8
Learn, Grow, Reap

Alexander the Great valued learning so highly that he used to say he was more indebted to Aristotle for giving him knowledge than to his father Philip for life.
—Samuel Smiles

Learners for Life

NOTHING STAYS THE SAME

The greatest leaders are forever improving themselves by feeding their unquenchable craving for knowledge. These constant learners stay on top, increasing their aptitude and efficiency by reading, researching, asking questions of mentors and experts, attending seminars, listening to podcasts and always being receptive to new perspectives. Doing this is a way of life for them, and as with all personal and professional development, there will always be new skills to learn, and new opportunities to test them.

Growth is a conscious choice, and the best leaders are driven by the pursuit of knowledge regardless of the effects that knowledge will produce. They don't need a reason to learn. Former NBA superstar Michael Jordan once said that great leaders must earn their leadership every day, and continuous learning and staying ahead of the game play major parts in that endeavor.

LEADING QUESTIONS ABOUT LEARNING

Throughout their careers and lives, constant learners ask themselves:

- What do I need/want to learn?
- What leadership skills, strategic practices or management techniques will help me to be more effective?
- Who can assist me in learning these new skills?
- Do I need formal training?
- What experiences will help?
- How can I apply my learning?

READ UP TO KEEP UP

Leaders can increase their education through a variety of means, reading being one of the most efficient. Reading challenges the mind, introduces new concepts and perspectives, and broadens the scope and quality of interpersonal communication. I have friends in their eighties who have always been voracious readers.

A late bloomer, I was in my early thirties before the light went on for me. Even so, the many benefits paid off immediately, and I began my eternal search for more information and learning anything that'd help me become a better leader.

I read every spare minute, devouring three to five books per week and quickly surpassing any required reading I never did in high school. Just like the other muscles in our bodies, the brain can be improved by working it repetitiously. Thanks to technology, I can multitask by working out or driving, while listening to audio business books and book summaries on sites such as Blinkist.com.

Studies reveal that affluent people have reading as a pastime in common. Still, successful people don't just peruse anything, they are highly-selective and prefer to be educated over being entertained. According to Tom Corley, author of *Rich Habits: The Daily Success Habits of Wealthy Individuals*, people with salaries of $160,000 or more and a liquid net worth of $3.2 million plus, read for education, self-improvement and success. In contrast, people who earn $35,000 or less and have a liquid net worth of $5,000 or less read mostly for entertainment.

LIFE-LONG LEARNERS:

- acquire a greater ability to see opportunities for change and growth that others may miss or never notice at all.

- become more open to trying new things.

- experience a strengthening of character while acquiring new knowledge.

- continue developing, practicing and updating not only pertinent technical (or hard) skills but also soft skills, such as management style and interpersonal abilities.

- encourage others to pursue continuing education.

BACK TO SCHOOL

One of the most direct ways to expand your knowledge is by earning an MBA, and colleges and universities are making continuing education more accessible than ever before. Online classes, satellite campuses and distance education give more people a chance to fit learning into their busy schedules.

When faced with the choice of getting several hundred dollars per month to stay in high school or $1,000 plus to leave and play major junior hockey, my teenage self thought it was a no-brainer. Not one of my better decisions, it turned out. Short-term, I made money and turned pro. Long-term, at twenty-five I was looking for a job as a high school dropout, which isn't a good look on anyone's resume.

My lack of formal education affected career moves and decisions I made along the way. For instance, I turned down a chance to interview for a promotion at a large public company because one of my new duties would include presenting to Wall Street investors. I was keenly aware that I didn't have the typical qualifications to become the CEO of a high-growth public company. I understood that in the public markets, investors and people evaluating the company expected CEOs, especially acquired ones, to have impressive education, titles and resumes. I didn't have that, so I declined to interview.

If I had it to do over again, I would have gone to college, not only for the discipline of learning but also the opportunity to hang around others with similar business aspirations. Instead, I had to bully and fake my way through my early business years, enduring through sheer will until I finally learned a better way. Had I been exposed to other business majors in school, I would have developed a more powerful network much quicker than I did on my own. After all, you don't need to know everything in business, you just need to know people who do.

Practice What You Teach

Recent studies have shown that there's a disconnect between many academics and today's workplace. Without real-world experience in the subjects they're teaching, and having spent most of their professional lives in educational institutions, professors may not be teaching the skills that employers look for in graduates. Some education systems are paying attention to this, specifically in business, recognizing that business professors who've never had to make payroll or deal with employee issues are ill-suited to teach business classes. Now, universities are considering making work experience a prerequisite for teaching academics, so students are more qualified to find positions in the workplace.

YOUR WAY

Your learning style is an inherent ability based on the way your brain works, which is why not everyone learns in the same way. Serious learners need to find out which approach works best for them since it impacts the way they understand information and solve problems. It took me a long time to figure it out, which is one of the reasons why I didn't get my GED until age forty-four. I was so disinterested in school because it bored the crap out of me. As a result, I didn't apply myself, and despite being smart, I didn't get the grades I wanted.

By the time I decided to get my GED, I'd discovered how I learned best—self-paced, no one slowing me down or telling me to work faster. This time around, I earned almost perfect grades because I was more interested. It was a triumph to finally be able to learn. Andragogy, the science of adult learning, provides information regarding how adults think, comprehend, process and retain new material. Most of us do best with a unique blend of learning styles, but there's usually one dominant way. Knowing how you absorb information helps maximize not only how rapidly you learn, but also how pleasurable the process is for you. Whenever I coach people, I always inquire about how they learn and depending on their style make accommodations, for example, offering them audio recordings rather than sending emails.

There are three primary learning styles. You may have heard of them, but if you haven't taken the time to properly assess your preferences, learning may be more difficult than it should be.

1. **Visual learners** prefer looking at images, such as charts, pictures, videos, and reading as ways to take in information. It's often difficult for visual learners to listen to lectures or explanations (see: *bored the crap out of me* above), favoring instead face-to-face discussions and detailed note-taking for later review.

2. **Auditory learners** need the *tell me* instead of *show me* approach. Auditory learners absorb new material best by participating in discussions and lectures, reading aloud and listening to others' ideas.

3. **Tactile or experience learners** acquire information by doing, and through interactive involvement instead of sitting for long periods simply listening or reading. The manual act of writing things down or a physically demonstrated technique is often the ideal way for them to retain new information.

Sharing the Wealth... of Knowledge
LEARNING AS A TEAM SPORT

> The best way a mentor can prepare another leader is to expose him or her to other great people.
> – John C. Maxwell

I grew up thinking that hanging around with extraordinary people was the norm, and didn't truly understand the impact of learning from others until I found myself unprepared for a business career. Although I had many mentors during my sports career, I hadn't been raised in a business culture and lacked role models for career number two. Besides my mother, basically a rank and file employee at one company for a quarter of a century, all my examples were sports people who'd stumbled into business. That fact, along with having no formal education, prompted me to seek out the collective intelligence of peer-to-peer leadership groups.

Always a believer in the power of great networks, peer groups offered me access to resources I could have never gained on my own. Think about the power of a community of networks compared to one. If you have trusting relationships with people who all have individual networks of connections, you also have contact to their networks, which makes finding varied resolutions to problems much easier. Conversely, if you remain insular and never venture outside your own company, then you limit your scope of assistance and advice.

Now, with technology, professionals can multiply their networks rapidly by connecting with others on sites like LinkedIn, Facebook, Instagram and Indeed, and building a meaningful group of contacts, the importance of which cannot be understated. A solid network helps executives weather difficult times and businesses prosper. I may have missed out on the opportunity to network in college, but peer groups helped me catch up. Ultimately, learning from, and networking with, others formed the groundwork for what I based my entire career around.

EXPANDING HORIZONS

At thirty-six and still a green company president, I joined my first peer group of small business leaders. I listened to members speak in code—*EBITDA, DSO, AR, AP*[2]—and use other terms that were foreign to me. After admitting this fact out loud—and prompting laughs from the seasoned businessmen in the room, I went directly to my CFO and learned everything a CEO needs to know about finance. By the next group meeting, I understood the meanings of each term and how our company scored in all categories. Then, because I turn everything into a game or competition to help me stay engaged, I suggested that my peer group members hold a contest.

We decided to measure comparable key metrics for the coming year and see who did the best in the categories that I mentioned in Chapter 5, Keeping Score: revenue, net income, growth, SG&A, and employee and client retention. In fact, that's where my future indicators originated and how I developed my best practices. Whether you're running a landscaping company, a high-tech or publishing firm, business is business. They all involve people, planning and process and can compete across industries using consistent key metrics. I wasn't as big as I wanted

---

2 EBITDA: earnings before interest, taxes, depreciation and amortization (net income with interest, taxes, depreciation and amortization added back to it)
DSO: days sales outstanding (average number of days that it takes a company to collect payment after a sale)
AR: accounts receivable (money owed to a company by its debtors)
AP: accounts payable (money owed by a company to its creditors)

to be yet, but certainly just as good since I recall winning the most categories among my group members.

Subsequently, we took a relatively small company with under $3 million in revenue, and grew it into the industry's largest private company in Southern California. Next, we competed with other companies in our market segment and gained national acclaim as a best-in-class company, the top performance level in an industry, used as a benchmark to be equaled or exceeded.

After conquering the marketplace, I set my sights on being a dominant company in our industry. I realized that being in a peer group within my industry limited me to the issues and history of that industry, which could only get me so far. Many mature industries at the time (like the stale and declining office equipment business), lacked innovation and sorely needed an infusion of new ideas. I knew I had to expand my view and look beyond my little fiefdom and comfort zone if I wanted to enter the big leagues of business.

So, once my company outgrew the other members' companies, I left my peer group to join a group of CEOs with larger companies than mine. It was the *big-fish-small-pond* effect, which I first experienced in my hockey days going from captain of my Midget and Junior hockey teams to the kid with no credibility at the Junior A level, and again when I turned pro. Still, each time I moved up a class, it forced me to improve and stay involved. Likewise, stepping up to a peer group of extraordinarily successful CEOs from assorted industries and studying them mastering their crafts, multiplied my business knowledge exponentially. That growth wouldn't have been possible within a single, competitive, industry roundtable forum.

THAT'LL TEACH YOU

In peer groups, CEOs introduced me to valuable strategies and insight that upped my game. Here are two of the game-changing lessons that I now pass along to others.

1. Hearing a good idea is one thing but converting it into action is another. Years ago, in a 15-member peer group, I met a gentleman who was the VP of sales for one of the fastest-growing mortgage companies in the country. He did a presentation on recruiting and proposed that even when you think you have a perfect team, something always happens, so never stop recruiting. After all, perfect teams lose members, too, for a number of reasons. I immediately took his advice, adopted his policy and my company nearly doubled in size the following year.

2. In 1999, a financial services CEO in my group warned the rest of us about the market meltdown that would result from the dot-com bust projected to happen in 2000. Having learned how to stay open to new views and alternate perspectives, I heeded his counsel and prepared my company for tough times. While other companies struggled, we experienced prosperous times from 2000 through 2005.

NEW PERSPECTIVES ON NEW INITIATIVES

Peer groups made me try harder and cured me of my tunnel vision by providing me opportunities to adopt and implement innovative ideas from others driven to be the best. Once I started paying attention to what other people were doing, I heard fresh, viable concepts that inspired me to ask myself, *Can I apply them in my business?* Then, I reached out to the CEOs who shared the innovations and asked them to coach me while I practiced the applications.

CEOs and entrepreneurs (especially early in their careers) are infamous for hearing an idea at some seminar or meeting, then acting on it without appropriate planning or follow-up with someone who's actually tried it. Needless to say, that way doesn't normally lead to long-term results. I'm as guilty as anyone for thinking of, or hearing about a new initiative and jumping in with both feet without forethought or capital. I've been caught up in *the flavor of the month.*

As entrepreneurs, we get excited about new notions, or *flavors,* and immediately employ them. In an effort to be progressive, CEOs get sidetracked by shiny objects and newfangled concepts. I've overheard senior executives of major companies practically praying that their bosses wouldn't announce another left field idea that's virtually impossible to implement.

Jim Freeman, the CEO of Day Runner back then (remember those once-ubiquitous paper planners?) and one of my business coaches, was the one who told me that there's a process for accomplishing anything. He taught me how to assess and test new ideas before employing, implementing or applying them, and how to present them to people and write plans properly. And, he showed me how to increase the odds of success by getting buy-in, or commitment, before presenting a new program or strategy to a company or sales team.

Jim was also the moderator of our group's business forum that consisted of a dozen ego-driven, A-type, control freaks. Still, within every group is a hierarchy of leaders and our club of 12 was no different. Whenever Jim wanted buy-in for a new initiative, he approached the highest-ranking leaders first, particularly the CEO who he knew would object the loudest. Even if Jim couldn't acquire buy-in, he knew that the loud CEO wouldn't be as reactive when the initiative was introduced to the entire group since he'd already been informed. Learning that preemptively informing a select few and accumulating buy-in before meetings benefited me whenever I needed alignment within my own companies. Furthermore, I learned that CEOs don't like surprises, and above all, want to be heard.

Before introducing a new initiative, leaders should consider the following questions.

1. **Was there enough advanced thought, planning and testing?** Trying something once (whether it works or not) isn't a sufficient test case, so I developed the following metrics. I test something 10 times and if it works six times there's hope, but, if it's successful eight times then I've got a bonafide triumph. In my younger days, I might try something once, and if it failed I'd

move onto something else. Extremely rigid in my ways as a young manager, I discovered in peer groups a better way than the hard way and enduring all kinds of failures. Peer groups encouraged me to be more flexible and more patient.

2. **Is there 100% internal buy-in prior to launching?** It's highly unlikely to get 100% buy-in for anything, but you still need significant commitment from your team. Before presenting anything, start engaging key people and gaining their trust by addressing potential obstacles or concerns and offering plans to combat them.

3. **Are we spending enough money on training and marketing to launch our initiative?** Research reveals that while most executives know that their company's progress depends on innovation, the majority of them admit that they commit insufficient resources to support new products and services. Without advanced planning, adequate funding and total commitment, it's not surprising many initiatives fail.

4. **Are we measuring progress over a sufficient time period and with enough customers to measure accurate results?** When we used to spend money on mailouts, newspaper, TV and radio, the results were fairly easy to measure within a few months. Nowadays though, with social media, search engine optimization (SEO), search engine marketing (SEM), and other web initiatives, results may take longer to achieve. In

a quick-changing world, what works today, may not work tomorrow.

General Exception to Buy-ins

I can think of only one person to get away without securing a buy-in for a new initiative and that's General George S. Patton. He ordered his troops to attack, and even his admission of certain and numerous casualties deterred neither his soldiers nor him from executing his plan. That's called blind loyalty. In business, that doesn't fly (see: Theranos).

A SAGE DECISION

By my mid-forties, after buying and selling several companies, the student became the teacher. Several CEOs who I admired (some with Harvard MBAs and others with bigger companies than mine) began asking me to coach them outside of the peer group. Still running a company, I counseled them at first informally like friends, but soon it became clear that I had processes, instincts and ideas that other CEOs didn't.

I didn't form Rollins Consulting Group until the demand was so high that I needed to do it for tax purposes. Within ninety days of hanging my shingle I had twenty clients who needed my help. It was my wife Terrie who suggested that I divide them into forums of people, which I did. Instead of counseling them one-on-one at high fees, I charged a lesser amount per month and put members in a room with 12 colleagues. It was a community of owners, CEOs and other C-level executives who all faced common business challenges, and I had them coach each other. I certainly didn't have all the answers and now I didn't have to work as hard. That's when I moved the majority of my clients from Rollins Consulting forums to my new company, Sage Executive Group. Since then I've coached hundreds of CEOs for companies in the $1 million to $3 billion revenue range.

Just as business leaders need to be selective with their hires, peer groups should be selective with their members—not exclusionary, but selective. Many groups let anybody in. In other words, if you can pay you can join. Generally, those groups fill up with mostly non-committed members with company-paid memberships and have horrible turnover ratios. There are other groups that reject many good people arbitrarily like an antiquated country club or a snobby fraternity (i.e. if the powers that be like you, you're in). I knew there was a better way.

What set Sage apart from other peer groups began with its members. They're all A players still in the game, and serious about the process. Only once in a while do lifestyle business owners slip through Sage's membership committee. Since these owners are content with how things stand and don't strive to grow, they tend not to add much to peer groups. More often than not, these CEOs deselect themselves and find other organizations more social in nature.

Other peer-to-peer platforms allow unqualified "coaches" to become leaders of their forums. Mid-level marketing managers who may be good recruiters have no business advising CEOs about big business without walking in their leather loafers (or high heels). Sage's measure of success for its coaches is financial independence—leaders who don't have to work but love giving back and helping others achieve their goals. Those are the people my partners and I put into chair positions. In addition, Sage's forums are member-focused and not driven by the financial need of the corporation.

A BAKER'S DOZEN OF CEOS

> **You are the average of the five people
> you spend the most time with.**
> **–Jim Rohn**

We took Jim's statement to a higher level and decided on thirteen, the size of Sage groups. I believe that's the magic number for CEO communities. Simplistically, in a group of five, two will be excellent, two will be average and one may not be active. However, utilizing the same percentages with a group of thirteen, you'll have a much better chance of always having the knowledge needed in a meeting to address any challenge members face.

Group Lessons

MENTORING IN THE WORKPLACE

Mentoring sometimes occurs spontaneously on the job, but owners who establish a more formal peer mentorship program gain tremendous value in long-term employee growth. In fact, a Deloitte survey of millennials found that the ones who planned to stay with their employers more than five years were twice as likely to have mentors (68%) than not (32%).

Mentoring in the workplace is a mutually beneficial practice for both parties. Within the Fortune 500 companies of today, about 71% of the companies have formalized mentoring programs. Here are some of the many benefits to employing an official mentoring system:

- It offers employees ongoing support and encouragement to improve their skills, navigate their careers and network within the organization.

- Workplace mentoring is an established technique for developing in-house talent and honing leadership capabilities.

- Employees who participate in mentoring programs report higher job satisfaction and therefore, better engagement and productivity.

- For many organizations, the knowledge of key individuals is their most valuable asset. Without an effective mentoring program, when these key individuals leave, their knowledge and skills go with them.

- Like an employee development program, a proven mentoring program is often used as a recruiting tool.

THE CALL TO MENTOR

No man is capable of self-improvement if he sees no other model but himself.
—Conrado I. Generoso

In general, true leaders will always give of themselves to others and want to share their knowledge. Therefore, when I first became a leader, I was never afraid to call or contact other leaders I didn't know. I'd explain that I'm a little startup in town and heard amazing things about what they've accomplished and wanted to learn from them. All but one CEO talked to me.

Coincidentally (or not?), later in my career we offered the same CEO who wouldn't talk to me millions to buy his company. Not only did he turn us down, but he also told me that he intended to own our company before long. Two years later, we bought his company for much less pre-bankruptcy. I'm not saying these two things are related, but… yes, I am.

SELECTING MENTORS & PEER GROUPS

Gretzky's mentor was his dad Walter, who trained and taught him until Wayne left home to play hockey. Walter touted hard work as the answer to success and Wayne immersed himself in the sport he loved and later in business. For those people who need to look beyond their gene pools for role models, it's important to think carefully about what you're looking for. *Do you want someone to expand your network of industry connections or simply be a sounding board? Who would best complement your personality and communication style?* A mentor in the same industry is fine, but effective mentoring bonds don't depend on it.

When asking someone to mentor you, be honest about what you hope to gain from the relationship. Looking for someone with a well-known name isn't as important as finding someone who you genuinely respect and has attained the kind of career and personal life you'd like to have. Consider asking a candidate for advice on one issue and evaluate it before committing. Think in terms of current development needs rather than future ones, keeping in mind that the same mentor who can support you today may not have the skills to help in five years. Though the friendships often endure long after the coaching ends.

Check out more advice for peer group beginners.

Choosing a peer group: Choose a group that fits your values, challenges you, and is meaningful to you both personally and professionally. The best peer groups focus on the whole individual, not strictly on achievement in business. Being a well-rounded, healthy and happy person is the true measure of making it. Highly-productive groups consist only of members who respect each other's experience and are eager to learn from one another.

Signs you've outgrown a group: Always stretch yourself to hang out with better, smarter and more experienced people.

When you surpass the average level of member expertise or think you're the smartest person in the room, you've outgrown your group. It's time to seek a new one with companies similar in size or at the same stage of development as yours, and members who inspire you. (*Cautionary note:* If you *always* think that you're the smartest person in every room then you're most likely delusional, in which case please stay away from all groups.)

Choosing who to mentor: Eventually in a mentor-mentee relationship, the one being mentored becomes a mentor in his or her right and will be sought out by others. Whenever I'm considering someone to mentor, I try to avoid people who are searching for quick fixes or magic formulas to grow their business. They tend to bounce from coach to coach, and peer group to peer group, never finding their answers. After all, you're giving up your time to spend it on someone else, so don't waste it on a person unworthy of investing in.

Before taking someone on, consider asking potential candidates to prepare presentations about their areas of expertise. I think it takes about a year to begin to have an impact on someone in business and life, so choose only those with shared values, who are coachable and committed. Mentees need to be open to trying new tools and strategies that mentors propose.

COMMUNITY KNOWLEDGE

When buying, selling or growing my companies (or facing other fundamental issues of a business owner) I relied upon group members, who became my trusted advisors—and lifelong friends. They helped me make much more money than I could have on my own.

The following are the most common CEO challenges discussed in peer groups and the leading corresponding advice.

Achieving work-life balance (aka *How to have a successful business and happy family life without dropping dead of a heart attack in the process*)

Work-life balance is among the most challenging aspects of being a busy professional. That's why it's necessary to plan for all aspects of your life, setting aside hours for work, family, hobbies, physical fitness, relaxation and even allowing time for emergencies. At a retirement ceremony in one of my first peer groups (which retired their members at 50), I sat among business legends. They had all made significant amounts of money, gained recognition and built empires, but the overwhelming majority also shared similar regrets—having caused their marriages to end and/or missing out on family time because of busy work schedules.

Whenever I considered taking a new position, I remembered what those retiring CEOs had said about not spending enough time at home and messing up their marriages. If they had a chance to do it again, my mentors would have chosen to have fewer corporate achievements and made more of an effort to keep their relationships intact. That had quite an impact on me. Even when I stood to make life-altering money for a role that most people would have jumped at, I knew it wasn't worth destroying my life for. For instance, traveling 250 days a year no matter how prestigious the job, would have taken a huge toll on my health and marriage—and I wasn't willing to risk either one. Not only did I fully understand that profound message, but I also continue to pass it along to other new entrepreneurs trying to balance their business and personal lives.

BUYING AND SELLING COMPANIES

Having a disciplined set of criteria, or a process in place for buying and selling is priority number one. Number two is having a strong team (including investment bankers familiar with your business and industry) and other behind-the-scenes advisors, such as a CFO (internal or outsourced), mergers and acquisitions (M&A) attorney and an experienced business advisor.

If you're planning to sell, you need tax, estate and wealth planning in advance. Wealth planning is a mix of tax planning, wealth protection, estate planning and business succession planning. When I first got equity in a business, it was *phantom equity*, which was taxed at a much higher rate than real stock at the time the company was sold. If I had done advanced financial planning I could have retained more of the proceeds. It's not what you sell a company for that matters, it's what you receive after taxes. That was an expensive lesson.

PARTNERSHIPS

Despite the fact that 70% of business partnerships ultimately fail (and 50% of partnerships fail within the first two to three years), many companies don't have clarified, documented arrangements in the event issues arise between partners.

Partnership agreements should include the following:

- A buy-sell agreement
- Insurance in the event of a partner's death or disability
- A clear delineation between ownership and daily operating roles (which needs to be reviewed and adjusted yearly)
- Voting rights
- A process for dealing with disagreements, such as arbitration or mediation
- Specific directives regarding balancing workload, boundaries, compensation, and what happens if unexpected change occurs
- Financial goals
- An exit plan that is agreed upon in advance

RAISING CAPITAL FOR GROWTH

Growth capital is intended to enable a company's accelerated growth through expanding operations, entering new markets or facilitating acquisitions. Here are the typical sources:

- **Friends and family.** They have always been the best source for raising money for early-stage companies.
- **Private equity.** This is a good option if you want to grow and still maintain partial ownership in the business without selling it all. Private equity firms generally want a large minority ownership stake in the business

in exchange for the growth capital and professional management they bring to the table.

- **Banks.** No two businesses are alike, so owners must choose banks according to their individual needs. Does a small community bank or a large national bank make more sense? For example, small banks may be more advantageous for new local businesses because they have less stringent requirements for opening accounts and lines of credit. Business loans from banks offer surprisingly great terms and interest rates depending on credit profiles and collateral. Other things to consider: lending capacity, business bank account rates, extra banking features and services.

- **Employee Stock Ownership Plan (ESOP).** An employee stock ownership plan isn't only a source of capital, but also a tax-advantaged way to transition ownership. It's a good option for private business owners seeking capital outside of family. Providing employees with stock ownership, companies contribute shares directly to the plan, or the plan borrows money to buy shares. If the plan borrows money, the company makes payments to the plan, so it can repay the loan.

MOVING PAST FEAR AND MAKING DIFFICULT DECISIONS

Stuff happens. The issue isn't what occurs, but rather how it's dealt with. The decisions that are most difficult versus the easy remedies are often the best long-term decisions, even though most of us would rather avoid doing the tough stuff. Here's how I learned to make decisions on important matters that have potentially detrimental consequences.

1. *Is the decision important right now?* If not, I don't act yet.

2. If the issue arises multiple times and has financial or cultural implications, I act.

3. Next, I gather input from as many parties as possible and determine which is the best long-term resolution.

4. Lastly, when I execute changes, I communicate them to all pertinent parties.

CHAPTER 9
Business Exit Strategies

What's your Endgame?

WORKING *ON* OR *IN* THE BUSINESS?

> Surround yourself with great people;
> delegate authority; get out of the way.
> –Ronald Reagan

Entrepreneurs, owners and leaders are control freaks by nature. They often get caught up in the day-to-day minutiae, or *working in the business*, and don't spend enough time looking at the bigger picture. However, before an exit strategy is contemplated, companies have to run themselves. To do that, the right people must be trained to carry out all duties and aspects of company business plans without relying on the owners.

Once that happens, principals can disengage and step back from everyday operations to concentrate on the company's long-term growth and future vison.

If a business can't operate or grow without its leader, then it's not a saleable asset regardless of how profitable it is. It's only when it achieves this stability and can exist without the top dog that a company has any great capital value. This transition is referred to as *working on the business.*

Working IN the business means:

- seeing clients and dealing with customers
- being the only rainmaker and producing most of the revenue
- invoicing clients
- answering queries
- tracking work in progress
- writing programs
- paying invoices
- preparing proposals
- handling crises

Working ON the business means:

- getting more education—from business blogs, podcasts and publications, peer groups, networking, industry events

- creating new processes and systems

- re-examining short- and long-term goals by planning for future expansion

- developing new marketing strategies, and updating social networking sites and promotion materials with current goals, products and services

- spending most of your day coaching and developing your leaders

MIND YOUR BUSINESS

Starting a business includes planning with the end in mind. As counterintuitive as that may sound, at some point, most businesses are either going to be sold or go through a transition. If there's a clear blueprint in place that structures the company to run independently, it's an easy shift. Alternatively, waiting until that time to devise an exit is virtually impossible because selling a business successfully takes time, and a great deal of planning—and it affects many people, which owners often underestimate. Owners who scramble to devise plans while trying to sell their companies won't fool buyers with irrelevant and slapdash versions.

A UBS Investor Watch survey revealed that 48% of business owners don't have formal exit strategies. Planning to run their businesses for the unforeseen future, many owners put off thinking about the end—however, things change quickly in business and life, and being caught unprepared (especially when there's hard-earned money involved) can be devastating both financially and emotionally.

ALL EXITS ARE NOW CLOSED

Studies indicate that seventy-five percent of business owners who have left their businesses wind up unhappy within a year of the exit for reasons which include:

- The company was undervalued.

- The seller paid too much in capital gain or estate taxes.

- The seller failed to realize financial or business goals because he or she hadn't planned beforehand.

- The seller no longer had a purpose or focus. Many former owners who always dreamed of selling and getting the money they wanted didn't bargain for what came with it—or what didn't. For some, the absence of daily challenges, interaction with great people, and a feeling of worth or purpose are unforeseen byproducts of the sale. For those ex-owners, choosing what golf course to play just doesn't yield the same power or rush as running a multi-million-dollar company.

MAKING AN EXIT

Certain exit strategies only make sense for certain types of businesses. This depends on a company's operational and financial transferability status, and the owners' personal goals. *Are owners planning for a huge payoff then setting sail into the sunset? If they stay with the company after it's sold, what do they want their roles to be? If they don't, who are their successors and why will they remain engaged?* Owners need to carefully consider all scenarios, how the transition will happen, and the steps involved.

- **Who will be the buyer?** Someone outside the industry, a competitor, a young entrepreneur?

- **Why will someone buy the company?** For the customer base, revenue, intellectual property?

- **How will buyers get a return for their investments?** When investors buy companies, they normally do so with the intention of recouping their investments through the growth of the business. Owners need to be prepared and understand what buyers will want to know. ROI (return on investment) and ROE (return on equity) are both measures of company performance and profitability. ROI measures the payback, forecasts the cash flow of the acquisition versus the initial investment, and calculates the rate of return. The ROI formula is *gain from investment* minus *cost of investment* divided by the *cost of investment* and multiplied by 100 as the results are a percentage. ROE calculates how much profit a company can generate based on invested money, and the basic formula is *net income* divided by *shareholder equity*. ROE can be used for comparing profitability of companies and factoring in debt. Both calculations used together can be strong indicators of investment profitability. Besides looking at a company's projected financial growth, buyers also consider things such as the proprietary technology a company owns or licenses, the financial and/or legal risks a company may face, the expertise of the management team and a company's prospects and opportunities for additional financing. During a recent buying frenzy with often ridiculously inflated prices being paid for companies, I wonder if buyers seriously considered how they'd recoup their investments and get the returns they expected or if they planned to wait longer for payback. If they didn't, they could wind up dumping their assets when there's an economic correction, leaving an excess of bargains on the market.

- **What can owners expect if they remain with the acquiring company?** When owners stay with companies post-acquisition, their time there may be temporary for many reasons, including the following. (*Note:* Founders who are part of the acquisition often do remain long-term, but they're the exceptions.)

  1. When big companies experience any economic downtown, the acquired, highly-compensated leaders are the first to go.

  2. Entrepreneurs who have never been accountable to boards or bosses are sometimes incapable of working for others... which is why they're entrepreneurs.

3. It's not uncommon for acquired leaders to realize (once they have plenty of money in the bank) that they don't want to work any longer—increased age and decreased motivation also could be factors.

4. Changes in the parent company's leadership can result in the new team bringing in their people and leaving former owners out.

5. The most common reason is that buyers and sellers set unlikely goals that can't be delivered during the acquisition process. For instance, if an earn-out—a financing arrangement in which a seller finances a portion of the purchase price and the buyer's payments depend on future business performance—is based on unrealistic earnings, changes in leadership are inevitable. (Whether in sports or business, it's always easier to change the coach instead of all the players.)

- **Is the leadership team prepared to run the company in the owner's absence?** Having a succession plan is vital, especially when there's a large investment involved. Companies must develop good succession plans that include either someone who can take over every key position at any time or a strong team or bench of leaders ready for the transition. Even if owners never plan to sell their businesses, taking this step affords them more time for family and a balanced life.

Passing the Business Baton

One of a true leader's last duties is recognizing when it's time to move on. So many athletes stay past their prime because they don't want, or know how, to do something else, or because the money is too good to give up. The worst examples of this are in family businesses that are doing well but could be doing even better. Founders stay too long because they don't have a succession plan in place with training for new leadership, or their identities are so connected with their businesses they can't see themselves doing something else. In other words, they can't separate despite it being in the company's best interest. Oftentimes, these businesses are overdue for an infusion of innovation.

I met Frank Greinke (god rest his soul), CEO of SC Fuels in my first business forum. In his prime (and after years of planning for the transition), he handed the CEO reins of one of the industry's biggest, private U.S. companies to his son Steven. A parent who believed his children should know every part of the company, Frank had Steven fulfill many roles before he felt his son was ready. Frank didn't need to step down but knew that after working hard for thirty-plus years, it was time to back out of the daily workings and enjoy his life. He also wanted the next generation to lead (out from behind his accomplished shadow) and welcomed his new role as chairman and go-to advisor for Steven.

A Way Out

KNOW WHAT YOU'RE GETTING INTO... BEFORE GETTING OUT

Planning early with different exit strategies allows owners the flexibility to get the most out of their business when it's time to get out.

GOAL: Acquisition

PLAN: Prepare for the tax and financial management required for a sale. I recommend that companies have financials that are GAAP-compliant reviewed for at least three years prior to sale. Utilizing outside consultants helps make sure that documents stand up to buyers' scrutiny. I don't think private companies need audited financials because it's more detailed and expensive and most acquiring parties do their own audits during due diligence—however, all public companies require audited financials.

Whenever possible, owners should hire established investment bankers who know the business, can obtain the best terms and navigate any obstacles. Small businesses that can't afford top-level CFOs can retain fractional CFOs (experienced senior-level executives) to advise them quarterly. It's money well spent. Temporary CFOs help with all aspects of moving companies forward, including grooming managers for increased responsibility when they're promoted. The additional resources and aid also mean fewer distractions for the management team. The process is a big undertaking, so owners must ensure alignment and transparency among board members, key stakeholders and management by keeping them informed throughout the process. Last-minute surprises or disagreements can delay an acquisition or cause it to fall through.

GOAL: Navigating unsolicited offers

PLAN: Sellers beware. Most businesses get unsolicited offers when they haven't yet decided to sell or prepared their businesses for sale. So, whenever I get calls from clients who have received unsolicited offers without competing offers, it concerns me. Sometimes rookie owners see letters of intent (LOIs) and start mentally retiring, becoming emotionally invested in selling. Often though, these buyers, who are more informed about a company's value than the majority of the business owners they approach, hope to get big discounts on companies. To that end, they may have simultaneously contacted numerous other owners, making low-ball offers and hoping that one sticks. Or they may want to acquire the businesses' intellectual property, which is why buyers should sign confidentiality agreements.

Smart sellers predetermine the purchase price they'd accept, and if unsolicited buyers aren't prepared to provide LOIs at that level, sellers shouldn't proceed. Unsolicited buyers are identified in the M&A process, so sellers also shouldn't sign an LOI before proper due diligence and professional valuation. An LOI usually provides buyers 60 days of unfettered access to company books during due diligence, when sellers aren't permitted to entertain other offers. The longer it takes, the bigger the toll on a seller's time and resources. The buyers, then in the power position of knowing a seller has no other options, often lower their bids, or attempt to retrade the original purchase price.

When a sale is managed correctly with investment bankers, and the financials and other preparations have been done, companies will be exposed to countless authentic potential buyers. With only one buyer, deals commonly fall apart. Those that don't often have sale prices lower than initial offers. With more buyers in the running, however, the prices go up. And with proper screening, sellers end up with lots of offers, allowing them to select the right price, terms and fit.

GOAL: Pass the business to the next generation

PLAN: Well in advance of the transition, the next generation needs the support of great role models and mentors within the company besides their parents. When the parent-owners have been the only mentors, the shift of power could be a rocky one—affecting family dynamics. Ideally, budding-CEOs are assigned internal, non-family mentors within the business long before they take on leadership roles. Then, when they do assume control, new leaders should be paired with trusted outside leadership advisors to further mentor them. Having professional coaches or business advisory boards that work with families throughout the process to help everyone stay on track, keeps both the companies and families intact.

GOAL: Train someone to run the company

PLAN: Many current-day entrepreneurs start companies then immediately incentivize and train others to run them so they can focus on multiple different ventures. One owner I know who planned to leave a business, groomed a young man coming up through the company ranks by sending him to the University of Southern California for an MBA, then Harvard for another degree and teaching him the skills necessary to take over.

GOAL: Transitioning a multi-generational company that never plans to sell outside the family

PLAN: For the company to continue successfully, a blend of key non-family, senior-level leaders should be retained, trained and fairly compensated to stay with the company. In some cases, that means giving them a share in the profits and/or retirement plans to secure them long-term. Having non-family members involved in senior leadership roles benefits owners by ensuring a broader talent pool.

GOAL: Sell or diversify a family-owned company

PLAN: If a family business is planning to sell for maximum value, it's important to identify the non-family successor and develop him or her into the leader who will continue with the business. Putting an objective, non-family leader in place operating independently from the core business provides objectivity when considering new opportunities. In my first equity role in a family business, this was the position I served long-term after the initial sale of the business.

There are advantages to diversifying a family business and providing alternative income independent of the main business. Risk management is the primary benefit because it helps ownership cover its bases by investing in different areas that will react differently to the same event. That makes owners feel more protected than being entirely committed to one business.

CHAPTER 10
The Stages of Success

There are no secrets to success. It is the result of preparation, hard work, and learning from failure.
— Colin Powell

Success & Significance

WHAT IS SUCCESS?

The meaning of success supports countless definitions mainly because the concept is deeply linked to a person's values and beliefs and therefore, highly personal. If you think having money is the most important thing in life, then you'd call material gains success. If your value system says that tranquility, stability or integrity are more important, then that's success to you.

Success could be changing behaviors (such as the move to living a healthy lifestyle) and attitudes that once held you back, or maybe it's simply doing the right thing when no one's looking.

Having a company that grows a little every year may mean success to some, yet to others it's developing a company that's the industry's best. Since success is also influenced by how people view themselves, their upbringings and relationships, it may even be one thing at a certain time in their lives and something entirely different at another.

My dad, for instance, longed for the fame and fortune of his NHL days. To him, that was success. Though he experienced business success after hanging up his jersey, it just wasn't the same as hockey, and hockey was his passion. Success to me (among other things) is having people who trust me and know that they can depend upon me and vice versa. No matter what success means to you, once it's attained comes the moment of truth when you'll ask yourself: *Is it everything I dreamed it'd be?* The answer might surprise you.

MOVE THE GOAL LINE

Early in our twenties, my wife and I decided what we wanted out of life and then determined how we'd get there. The magic number was $X million, and there was a science behind it. The actuary tables said we'd likely live to be eighty-four to eighty-eight so if we had no debt, our spend level didn't surpass X-amount per year and we accumulated $X million in money and equity, we'd be able to retire in our forties. Then, if we invested our money wisely after that, we told our younger selves, we'd never have to work again. We wrote that formula down and still have the piece of paper.

Right on schedule during my forty-fourth year, we achieved success by selling our company—our long-ago chosen goal—and I was totally unfulfilled. *I made it, so now what?* From this new vantage point, twenty-plus years down the road from when I first plotted to achieve the things I thought mattered, my choices suddenly seemed so shortsighted. Having financial independence didn't mean what I envisioned it would.

That's when I started thinking about the rest of my life's plan. I considered deeper, more profound things than how much money I wanted to make and reevaluated my definition of success. *How did I want to be remembered?* After all, you can be rich, but if you're not remembered, what did you really achieve? *Who am I now? What kind of a husband am I and can I improve? What kind of impact can I have on my community?* These were the questions my more-mature self pondered.

I also had another epiphany. What I thought were both finish lines—making it to the major leagues in hockey and achieving my monetary goal in business—existed solely in my mind and weren't finish lines at all. In fact, they were the next *starting lines*. The only *real* end lines are when you give up… or die. Since neither of those applied (or appealed) to me, I chose to move the line instead, and begin another quest toward a new goal: becoming my most-fulfilled *me*.

SOWING THE SEEDS OF SUCCESS

Mapping out a plan and deciding what success really looks like *before* journeying to achieve it, prevents you from later discovering that it's not what you wanted after all. The sooner you begin, the closer you'll be to living the life you truly desire.

First, take inventory of who you are and what you want by exploring the answers to these questions:

- *What matters to you? (What are you passionate about?)*

- *What lifestyle do you want to attain?*

- *Who do you want to be? (Characteristics and values.)*

- *What do you want people to recall about you after you die? (What kind of legacy do you want to leave?)*

Next, firm up an action plan with steps toward success.

1. Write down three things that you most want to achieve. Be specific and include what the achievement of each looks like and the reasons why it's important to you.

2. Break every goal into smaller, achievable objectives. Figure out what you want to deal with first then take them one at a time, setting realistic deadlines.

3. Study people who have accomplished what you want to do. *How did they succeed? How long did it take? What skills do you need?*

4. Measure progress frequently, to stay on track, and celebrate milestones toward success.

5. Join a peer group or find a mentor, someone willing to listen, offer advice and provide encouragement. *Is there anyone else you need to enlist?*

TURNING SUCCESS INTO SIGNIFICANCE

> Success is peace of mind which is a direct result of self-satisfaction in knowing you made the effort to become the best you are capable of becoming.
> – John Wooden

Not every successful person has significance, but every person of significance is successful. Success is your personal definition, whereas significance is the view of you that's held by others. Simply, success is getting, significance is giving. People who are striving for success are likely doing things for themselves, while people who strive for significance are focused on serving others. For instance, success is reaching your goal of becoming a CEO, but significance is coaching and assisting hundreds of CEOs.

Though a money-making enterprise, Sage Executive Group deliberately incorporates significance into its business plan. Every Sage forum helps promote a nonprofit, typically a regional, charitable foundation, such as Torrie Dunlap's. Propelled by her life's passion to help those less fortunate, Torrie joined Kids Included Together as CEO, a nonprofit that helps organizations meaningfully include kids with disabilities.

Sponsored by Sage, Torrie's permitted to hang out monthly with the best and brightest in business and receive invaluable help. Nonprofits still have to deal with the business end of their endeavors—such as fundraising, hiring, firing and protecting assets from lawsuits. Instead of just writing checks, Sage gifts time, knowledge and experience that the selected CEOs couldn't get anywhere else, increasing their chances for success and significance. When you connect with someone or enrich the life of another, then he or she influences the life of someone else, and so on, and your significance endures.

Success: At What Cost?

I met Ray Kroc, the late billionaire famous for growing and franchising McDonald's, through hockey. A huge hockey fan, he owned the WHA's San Diego Mariners and San Diego Padres. Still a milkshake machine salesman into his fifties, he didn't achieve monetary success until almost sixty. Despite his fortune, however, he faced many life challenges which were highlighted in the movie about his life. Undeniably, he made much more money than I did or ever will, but I'm definitely richer. For one, my incredible wife Terrie of four-plus decades—my greatest success (and significance), for sure.

Purpose & Mastery

ON PURPOSE

It is not enough to be industrious; so are the ants.
What are you industrious about?
– Henry David Thoreau

Whereas significance is the degree to which something matters, purpose is your passion's objective, an aim to be reached. Purpose is what drives you and fulfills you daily. Purpose is the most powerful motivation in humans, drawing on emotions and inspiring a higher level of commitment than fame, money or power. Discover your passion and start with purpose instead of money, and you'll never work another day in your life.

Our purpose and actions are a major part of what defines us. If you're not working toward a purpose, or making a difference in some way, you're likely allowing others to dictate your path instead of finding your own. Consequently, you wind up doing unfulfilling and often stressful work. The good news is that everyone can find purpose and bring it to their professional and personal lives.

Many fellow baby boomers, having begun their careers chasing the money, are looking for greater significance and purpose as their careers wind down. Interestingly, many millennials just beginning careers are looking for both. As much as millennials get a bad rap for being entitled, impatient and egocentric, they seem to me more balanced in their views on life and what's truly important compared to my generation.

The millennials I know are driven—working and playing hard. They're actually planning their lives and thinking about things—but not necessarily the things that appealed to my peers. They're renting longer, waiting it out until they can afford the real deal. Unlike their predecessors, millennials are also putting off wedding vows until they're older, not wanting to make the same mistakes their parents did (namely divorce). They're trying to do it right.

When it comes to purpose, business leaders need to ask themselves where they want to take their companies. *Do they want to be the biggest or the best? Do they want to excel in services, products or both? Are their purposes clear? What do they want their companies' reputations to be? How must they conduct themselves to lead their organizations, motivate others and support their visions?*

PURPOSE-DRIVEN PERKS

- When purpose is clear it's easier to focus on what truly matters and decide where to spend the most energy, time and other resources.

- Purpose ignites perseverance and the courage to overcome obstacles and solve challenging problems; without it, unexpected changes can derail you.

- A compelling and clearly-defined corporate purpose can contribute up to a 17% improvement in financial performance in the short-term, and more down the line.

- Research shows that purpose-driven people are four times more likely to be engaged at work. They are 50% more likely to be leaders, have higher income and net worth, and experience 64% more career satisfaction than people who don't work toward a purpose.

MY PATH TO PURPOSE

As a partner in my third job, I started being recognized and appreciated for my contributions to a company for the first time. My partners gave me their full support, valuing everything I did and making sure I knew it. The positive reinforcement became the impetus behind my (long-resisted) belief in myself, and acknowledgement that I was truly good at my craft. That newfound confidence allowed me to get even better. I finally mustered the courage to unleash my real potential by putting into practice every process, system and idea that I promised myself I'd do one day when I owned a company.

I started building the positive and ideological culture that I'd always believed in, hiring A players, and getting rid of nonperformers and people who weren't on board. Rejecting authoritative management, I handed out positive affirmations generously and rewarded my managers by affording them the authority and autonomy to be happy within the company. In fact, after we sold our company, leadership scattered because they no longer had coveted autonomy—when it's taken away, people often go away too.

The win for me though, was seeing the fruition of my ideas, having the team share in the implementation of these plans, and making everyone feel like an owner. I still made mistakes, but my processes worked better than anywhere I'd been before. During this time, my purpose became clearer and clearer. It wasn't only executing my plans, but also sharing what I learned with other business leaders.

A Promise with Purpose

Once my attention turned to attaining purpose-driven goals, I began at the top of that list by fulfilling a commitment to my mom. I enrolled in night school and got my GED. It was important to her, but it was to me, too—for different reasons. Among them, when I write things down or make a commitment, I follow through. I surprised my mom with a photo of the diploma, and despite having to wait almost three decades, she was thrilled that I did it. So was I.

I also completed my long term commitment to write this book. This was something I wrote down as a goal in 1999 and finally got to in 2020. Better late than never!

START PURPOSELY

Business experts say that the majority of people start careers in the pursuit of money, which often evolves to pursuit of autonomy, followed by significance and hopefully, one way or another they arrive at purpose. Interestingly, phenomenal athletes and outstanding leaders reverse the order, starting and staying with a purpose, and the money, fame and the rest usually follow.

Wayne Gretzky's purpose was to be the best at whatever he pursued. I played with *The Great One* during his rookie year of professional hockey when he was 17, and he showed signs of his purpose and destiny even then. He was the first to work every day and the last to leave, striving relentlessly toward his goal, his purpose. People like my father, Wayne and Gordie never cared about the money because they would have played for free. They never swayed from their purpose to be the best at what they loved, and that's what made them great.

Those that begin with purpose also typically achieve great things more quickly than those who are originally motivated by money (or never move beyond it). They grow companies faster because they do things for the right reasons and don't abandon their purposes or sell out as soon as they get big. Purpose-driven companies achieve success while being personally meaningful and socially beneficial.

Stone Brewing (the ninth-biggest craft brewery in the U.S.) is a company I admire, and they are also part of the Sage community. They always focused on their customers and creating amazing products rather than the money. The owners concentrated on being the best they could be and stayed true to themselves as they grew. Many of their competitors sold out to Anheuser Busch, other giant brewers and corporations, or were unable to keep growing. Stone Brewing flourished and rose to the top of the industry.

During both sports and business, I (like most people) focused on earning a living upfront. Once I started to make money in business, however, autonomy became just as important to me. I craved the freedom to manage my calendar and remove myself from the demands that employees add to the equation.

I wanted anything I did to be virtual—no office, no permanent employees, no facilities, no daily demands.

Had I known what I know now, I would have committed to a purpose initially and had faith that the monetary success would eventually come. Leaders who aren't tied to a purpose, give up more easily during tough times and avoid taking risks that could lead to innovation. I would have risked venturing out on my own, becoming my own boss and creating my own culture and message much sooner instead of delivering on someone else's (which I didn't always agree with).

Purpose the Second Time Around

Dan Feder, like me, didn't start out with purpose-focused motivation. Fresh out of the University of Southern California, he and a friend started a finance company, which helped businesses acquire working capital, and earned spots (three different times!) on the INC. 500 list of America's fastest growing companies. As it turned out, however, Dan didn't share a passion for the business and made a career change before looking for a venture that inspired him. He switched gears and chose a business he truly loved. In his search, he discovered the multi-family apartment business and founded F & F Income Properties LLC, which he also successfully grew into a world class enterprise. This time around he found his purpose along with a venture that his children and their children could become involved in.

MASTERY AT ITS BEST

Becoming a master of any job means really learning it, studying it, and experiencing it. Most businesses do little to promote mastery and it's rarely a prerequisite for company advancement. Although a company can't force employees to become masters of their crafts, a progressive one creates a culture that encourages it. There's always more to know and room to grow.

Some of the best CEOs I know came from family businesses where it wasn't unusual for parent-owners to insist their offspring seek employment elsewhere before joining the family company. When the kids finally did come aboard, they didn't start as presidents, but rather chief bottle washers or floor sweepers. Their wise parents insisted that their progeny immerse themselves in the business and master it, starting at the back door before ascending to the executive suite.

Mastery isn't only committing to a goal, but it's also about the rewards in striving toward it. Simply putting in the time to get better and better at something that matters to you teaches you things like perseverance, discipline, patience, effort, intention and how to handle failure. Mastery provides unexpected opportunities for growth and self-discovery and makes you a better and quicker learner by uncovering how you learn best. It's a way to stretch your abilities by concentrating on the correct method rather than only the outcome. Those who have achieved mastery are the best in their fields, and therefore, (similar to purpose-driven achievements) success and all the trappings typically ensue.

Deciding on what to master can be based on skills you think will pay off in the future, or proclivities and abilities you already possess and want to keep improving upon. Once you decide, you'll know where to focus your attention. The most important part of mastery is practice, practice, practice. Along with honest feedback so that you know what to correct, reinforce or continue. Peers, mentors, masters, books, videos and more can provide guidance.

MASTERING THE GOOD LIFE

At 22, Swiss immigrant Stephan Goss founded Zeeto Media (a marketing data discovery company that experienced a growth rate of 98% within three years) which earned him a place on the *Forbes 2018 30 Under 30* list in Marketing & Advertising. Stephan never concentrated on attaining success and wealth, but instead on his purpose, building great companies that allowed him the flexibility to master what he loves. When he wanted to learn the game of polo, he took lessons with a polo master, bought a horse and joined a team. Next, he wanted to learn how to raise bonsai trees, and after that, to master indoor acrobatic skydiving. Stephan's idea of success is mastering his passions and fulfilling his purpose.

Leaders & Legacy

LEAVE A LOT TO BE DESIRED

Rich or poor, famous or unknown, everybody leaves behind a legacy—some decidedly more memorable than others. A legacy comes down to how people viewed you, how you inspired others, or how you made them feel in the workplace and in your off-hours. Some people inadvertently pass on their legacies without ever thinking about planning for it, while others deliberately map out and live accordingly to their chosen direction. Think of legacy as post-purpose. Those of us who strive toward a purpose while we're living carry hopes of creating a legacy that's worth leaving.

Legacies may be what we leave behind once we retire from a company—or this dimension. It's the passing along of talents, knowledge, core values and life experiences, and inspiring future generations. Unfortunately, in today's impersonal, technology-driven world, it's easy to lead (read: hide) behind emails and texts instead of taking the time to connect face-to-face, which hinders making consequential impressions on others. The most enduring and significant legacies are intentional and take time to build.

The reality is that most leaders don't leave legacies and therefore, once they exit an organization they're never heard from or mentioned again. However, for leaders who aspire to leave worthwhile legacies, it's never too early to consider this question: *Do I foster long-term advancement of company leaders? Have I improved hiring and development practices? Am I contributing to the greater good?* These are the types of accomplishments that produce remarkable, and continuing, legacies. Years from now, former team members won't remember whether or not their leaders hit their numbers, but they'll certainly remember whether they were tyrants or teachers.

Once leaders have clarity on their legacies, they can start planning for them just like planning for a purpose. This is done by setting attainable, measurable goals with deadlines and doing what matters *now*. Pinpointing a legacy provides direction and inspiration to achieve more, positively influencing day-to-day decisions. All actions that owners make not only have the power to contribute to the success or failure of the companies they built, but also to define their legacies.

Undoubtedly, the formidable accomplishment of raising good kids, who give back to their communities or the world, are profound and living legacies. However, for those of us without children (or buildings named after us) like Terrie and I, our legacies will be about living productive lives, setting good examples and contributing to others' growth. Knowing that someone will carry on something they learned from us means our time on earth was well spent.

I can remember exactly who taught me each concept I ever learned and it's my hope that by mentioning my mentors' names and crediting them, they live on through my generation and beyond (see: this book). What you pass onto others and they pass onto the next generation may not immortalize you, but it continues the ideas, plans and achievements worth preserving. Knowing that is its own reward.

I got to experience something most people don't. I eavesdropped on my eulogy (sort of). Several years ago, ten former coaching clients and their spouses hosted an *appreciation dinner* in my honor. One-by-one, they thanked me for helping them and making a difference in their lives and businesses. The CEOs, mostly in their thirties and forties, joked about the night being a pre-funeral since I was in my fifties and time was running out to express their sentiments about me and my legacy. It was very touching to be thought of in such a way, and a lot to live up to.

A NAME TO REMEMBER

A friend of mine, whom I admired greatly was a member of a third-generation, century-old business. A community college graduate and average student, he'd been chosen over brothers and cousins with degrees from prestigious universities to take the helm of one of the biggest national private companies in the industry segment. His visions were ahead of their time and the family recognized his innovation and other leadership qualities.

Visiting his office for the first time, I expected to find an interior-designed, palatial corner unit worthy of such a reputable CEO in the 1990s. Imagine my surprise upon seeing his nondescript cubicle in the middle of a cubicle farm. That same day, we also toured his giant facility in Los Angeles, California, which employed thousands of employees. Walking by the long assembly lines, he knew the name of every person we passed. That was his legacy.

BIG LEAGUE BOSSES SOUND OFF

What qualities do leaders need to succeed? Which characteristics help them to persevere, and ultimately, triumph in both business and life? What traits should young entrepreneurs look for when choosing leaders and team members?

Seven business big-leaguers each shared one leadership attribute that significantly helped them to achieve success throughout their careers.

Here's what they had to say.

ATTITUDE

Attitude, derived from one's outlook on the world, is a little thing that makes a big difference. I agree with evangelical Christian pastor and author Charles R. Swindoll who said, "Life is 10% what happens to you and 90% how you react to it." *I've subscribed to this belief system for years. It's also been scientifically proven that attitude is tied directly to health and wellbeing. Every day we receive thousands of pieces of information, which can be overwhelming at times if we let it. What I've found is that without a personal attachment to every piece of information or outcome, life happens as it should—most of the time.*

The best leaders demonstrate positive attitudes, which must be genuine and can't be faked. Fostering an optimistic outlook is a practice and a discipline for some. However, leaders who succeed, influence beneficial change in those around them. Leaders have the greatest influence on company culture, so it's up to them to carefully select team members who'll add value, particularly when they're faced with challenges and opportunities. Hiring with culture in mind and seeking those individuals whose attitudes reflect your company's, provides more value than any talent you can hire.

I've been constantly reminded of the power of attitude every week for the past twenty-five years, during team meetings when thirty-five of us share recent wins. Attitude is the driving factor behind each one.

Jennifer Miller joined Access Destination Services (a leader in the domestic Destination Management Company market) as a program manager and today she's the CEO. The company has doubled its business over the last five years under her leadership, steadily building on a foundation of best-in-class service that traces its roots back almost fifty years.

DISCIPLINE

I started my career as an accountant in a highly profitable office products company in New York. I was good at finance, but soon realized the path to top leadership was through sales. So, with the help of Bob Keck, (my mentor and the company president) I transferred to sales, where I learned discipline and strong, fundamental business practices, and experienced even greater success. Still, I didn't yet comprehend how valuable my early training in New York would be to the rest of my career.

In the late 1980s, hundreds of office products companies (including mine) were acquired by large conglomerates that enjoyed their rich margins but didn't fully understand the business model. As a result, most of the acquired management teams remained intact with minimal supervision. Our parent company's CEO, impressed with New York's performance, asked me to interview for a VP position at a recently acquired California company.

It didn't take long to figure out that the West Coast acquisition was a mess. The company did about $25 million in annual sales, but still managed to lose $2 million dollars every year. I planned on turning down the position, but when my CEO (who I trusted to have my best professional interests at heart) implored me to take it, I reluctantly accepted the challenge.

Once there, I met with management to determine exactly where changes had to be made. I quickly learned there was no plan—or process, metrics, deadlines, or accountability for any area of the business; in other words, there was no discipline. Not only did the senior staff ignore financial fundamentals, they also didn't understand their value, which the team's poor performance reflected.

Before long, I shared my findings with the CEO who'd urged me to take the job. I told him that no VP position would yield the power necessary to make a dent in the organization's litany of problems and therefore, I didn't want my name attached to a company about to implode. Agreeing with my assessment, he promptly fired the president, CFO & VP of sales and appointed me president.

I set the bar very high, but believed we could succeed by implementing tighter controls and disciplined plans in all aspects of the business. I refined my senior management team, met with each employee and clarified job descriptions—as well as department and company goals, and compensation and bonus opportunities (aka what was in it for them). We measured and managed everything daily, weekly, monthly, quarterly and annually, and consistently closed the books on time, which held everyone accountable.

Within a year, the California company turned around, thanks to a clear direction and new, disciplined systems. Over the next ten years, I repeated this precise and successful, fix-a-sick-company model many times, and by the time I retired from that company I'd managed over a billion dollars in annual revenue. In business as in most areas of life, there can be no long-term success without discipline.

Tom Deverell has assisted in the growth of both companies and individuals as a turnaround specialist for companies ranging from Fortune 500 companies to startups. As the Vice President of IKON Office Solutions, he was able to turn around underperforming companies that were struggling, and amplify the success for others that were already strong. He continues to leverage his acute vision for business strategy by coaching and mentoring CEOs and business executives, and serving as a facilitator chair for Sage Executive Group.

DRIVE

Leaders must be mentally strong. They have to be willing to risk failure—but more importantly—they have to be tough enough to fight back, endure and succeed the next time.

The most consequential event of my career happened in my mid-thirties, shortly after General Electric's board of directors made me a corporate officer. One day in a very public setting, I ran afoul of Jack Welch, GE's Chairman and CEO, who dressed me down about the performance of GE Medical Systems. He felt that I could, and should, be doing more for the business I ran. It was incredibly humiliating, and I thought my career was over.

The next day, I met with GE president (and future Chairman and CEO of GE) Jeff Immelt who'd already heard about the incident. Not only did he hear from my colleagues who'd witnessed it, but also from Jack who'd called to vent his frustration about a (former) wunderkind named Greg! Jeff, a terrific mentor, shared with me that he'd also once found himself on the wrong side of Jack. He counseled me to put my head down, keep a low profile, and just out-execute everyone around. In time, he said (emphasizing the word time) Jack would notice and respect me even more for sticking it out and not quitting. Jeff's exact words were, *Don't walk out the back door.*

I was never so driven to prove to myself, and the GE community, that Jack had been wrong in his assessment, and I redoubled my efforts. Still, it was a lonely time, feeling out of place at officer's meetings, and virtually isolated in my own company, until two years later and out of the blue, I got a call from Jack. He'd been watching, and impressed with the business I'd built, wanted me to be a featured speaker at the annual senior leadership meeting about lessons learned. I was back!

Leading through adversity and maintaining my drive (when the far easier path would have been to walk out the back door) impacted me greatly. Now, I'm thankful for that fateful day because it helped build the character required for me to achieve even bigger things.

Greg Lucier is the Chairman and former CEO of Nuvasive, Inc.($1 billion in revenue), the former CEO of Life Technologies (which sold for $15.6 billion), and former president of GE Medical Systems ($5 billion in revenue). In 2011, he was #12 on Forbes list of the highest-paid CEOs.

EMPATHY

Empathy, the ability to be compassionately responsive to the needs of others without losing one's own personal identity, is essential to leading others with integrity. Furthermore, since studies reveal that individuals are most empathetic to those most like them in ideology, gender and background, it takes special kinds of leaders, such as transformational servant-leaders, to remove their own contexts and accept individuals for their uniqueness. Those kinds of leaders can change the status-quo by playing a dramatic role in improving the lives of others while positively affecting the bottom line in business.

Servant-leaders are skilled empathetic listeners and see the good intentions of people. They're adept at recognizing emotions in others and reading subtle social signals of what people need or want. They don't reject others even when certain behaviors or performances are deemed inappropriate. Few reach that level of empathy, but those who do can help the hopeless become hopeful, the desperate to renew their dreams, and the lifeless begin to live life again.

Dr. Tony Baron is an associate professor of Leadership and Cultural Engagement at Azusa Pacific University and serves as Scholar in Residence at the Center for Executive Excellence in San Diego. He's also an acclaimed speaker, leadership consultant, executive coach, psychologist, theologian and author of The Art of Servant Leadership and many other books. Dr. Baron counseled survivors of the Oklahoma City bombing, the Columbine High School massacre, and the attack on The World Trade Center.

GRIT

When you leave home at a young age, as I did to play hockey, you quickly learn to fend for yourself, making decisions on your own and dealing daily with the fear of failure. You learn to deal and work with whatever you have, cherish and savor the little things you accomplish and never get complacent. You learn that excuses are irrelevant. You learn that you can't sit on the fence, and essentially have three choices: lead, follow or get out of the way. The choice is yours.

How did I make it? For me, the survival traits that I learned early on, along with the willingness to compete, and a never-be-satisfied attitude contributed to the success I experienced later in life. I believe that mustering the grit to accept and overcome difficulties and adversity, makes you truly appreciate success on a different level than those who haven't faced, and prevailed over, hardship.

In the competitive worlds of sports and business, finishing second just isn't good enough, so grit can be a game changer. But it isn't all about being physically tough. It's about attitude and state of mind. The pinnacle of my career, and the payoff for dealing with numerous setbacks head-on, was being named captain of the Detroit Red Wings (one of the original six NHL teams)—a title that must be earned and voted on by peers. Hockey taught me hard work, discipline, respect, honesty, appreciation, being humble and I'll always remain grateful and privileged to have played.

Dennis "Polo" Polonich is a retired professional ice hockey center who spent his entire professional hockey career with the Detroit Red Wings. Though fearless, Polo at only 5-foot-6 and 166 pounds, needed a way to get the attention of the pro scouts. He did so by becoming one of the most penalized players in hockey during both his junior and pro career. The Red Wings, looking to add more toughness and grit to its roster after a few disappointing seasons, decided Polo fit the bill. Despite his size, he played for 14 years.

HUMOR

I discovered very early in my career that having a self-deprecating sense of humor and being a nice person, paid big dividends. I'd even argue that tasteful humor serves as a strategic tool and can represent a distinct competitive advantage. Humor in business is disarming, enriching and motivating.

While humor won't likely solve difficult issues, it can clear the air of tension, spurring creativity, lowering barriers and opening up possibilities. Great leaders know when to deploy humor to rally the troops, humanize their lofty positions and make themselves more relatable. Cultural health and morale are directly impacted by the signals that management sends, and a collective or organizational sense of humor can be palpable. Customers, prospective employees and team members sense it and respond in kind.

Humor shouldn't diminish or mask the serious work at hand, but properly channeled, it can add levity and high spirits to a tense environment. It's not about telling jokes, or making light of a serious situation; rather, it's about setting a tone in an organization that maintains perspective and underscores enjoying the journey.

John Heffner has recently joined Summer Fridays as Chairman/CEO. Prior to this he had a successful exit as CEO of Drybar where under his leadership the brand experienced amazing growth in his 6 plus years. Formerly the president and general manager of OPI, and CEO of Creative Nail Design, he's a legend in the beauty products industry. John is also a past chairman of the Young Presidents' Organization (YPO) in San Diego, and recipient of the City of Hope's Spirit of Life award, one of the highest honors in the professional beauty industry.

KEEPING COMMITMENTS

One of the traits I valued most in a coach was the ability to keep commitments. Keeping commitments is important because that sets the tone for a general expectation of performance and creates a standard within a culture.

When team members buy into that standard, they'll literally alter their professional (and to some degree, private) lives, making any changes necessary to meet it.

A leader who doesn't keep commitments, for example by demonstrating constant tardiness, making unfulfilled promises or consistently changing the value system, is unaware of the power of leadership. A leader who can't keep his commitments doesn't value team members or recognize the inconveniences his irresponsibility poses for them, and impedes the progress of the team and therefore, the business.

Of course, life happens and plans change, so it's important to:

- *Be thoughtful and make only the commitments you're willing to work your hardest to keep.*

- *Renegotiate terms with your team and come to an agreeable medium whenever a commitment has to be broken.*

- *Regularly acknowledge your team for accommodating any changes that occur. Make sure your team feels that you never take their support for granted.*

Be a leader who keeps commitments!

Terrell Fletcher was an NFL running back for the San Diego Chargers for eight years. He's now a successful entrepreneur and speaker, and coaches business leaders on how to produce company wins. He's also an ordained bishop and senior pastor for City of Hope International

Church in San Diego, and in 2017 authored his first book, The Book of You: Discover God's Plan and Transform Your Future. A first-generation college graduate, Terrell has a bachelor's degree in English literature, a master's degree in religious studies and a doctorate in transformational leadership.

Ten Things I Learned… and Can Apply Today

	PG. #	PROCESS	NOTES/APPLICATIONS
1.	Ex.	Writing a plan	Write goals specific to each employee's role making clear how individual performance affects the organization.
2.			
3.			
4.			
5.			
6.			
7.			
8.			
9.			
10.			

APPENDIX

When compiling the resources for this section, I quickly realized that many of my recommendations for continued learning and useful apps and tools were online based. Given that I intend for this book to be an evergreen resource, I made the decision to have that evolving list live on my website so that I can ensure that what I am sharing is always current and valuable.

Please visit jerryrollins.com/tools to access my most current recommended resources and book downloads.

I have left the reading list below because books—of course—are timeless.

Recommended Reading:

The Go-Giver: A Little Story About a Powerful Business Idea by Bob Burg & John David Mann

Never Eat Alone and Other Secrets to Success, One Relationship at a Time by Keith Ferrazzi

Who's Got Your Back: The Breakthrough Program to Build Deep, Trusting Relationships that Create Success– and Won't Let You Fail by Keith Ferrazzi

Swim with the Sharks, Without Being Eaten Alive by Harvey Mackay

What Got You Here Won't Get You There by Marshall Goldsmith

Selling to Vito (The Very Important Top Officer) by Anthony Parinello

Analyzing Performance Problems by Robert F. Mager

Three Feet from Gold by Sharon L. Lechter and Greg S. Reid

The One Minute Manager by Ken Blanchard and Spencer Johnson

Topgrading: How Leading Companies Win by Hiring, Coaching and Keeping the Best People by Bradford D. Smart, Ph.D.

The 7 Habits of Highly Effective People by Steven Covey

We've Got to Start Meeting Like This: A Guide to Successful Meeting Management by Roger K. Mosvick and Robert B. Nelson

Additional Learning:

American Management Association (AMA), www.amanet.org

Suggested courses for staying on top in business:

- Strategic Planning
- Finance for non-financial managers
- Public Speaking
- Interpersonal Skills
- Time Management

ACKNOWLEDGMENTS

Most acknowledgments written by former male athletes or successful business people tend to focus on their fathers, star athletes, coaches and other male role models and mentors. I've been fortunate to have those in my life, but I chose to dedicate this book to three women who helped shape the man I am today.

My mother, Bertha, taught me about hard work during her successful 23-year career in business. I observed her mental toughness as she persevered through the trials and tribulations of raising two challenging teenage boys. These experiences showed me I should always do the right thing, even when faced with daunting or seemingly insurmountable challenges.

Betty Jean Jones, my mother-in-law, is the second recipient of my dedication. From her, I learned the fortitude and courage to face difficult times and raise a family successfully with a kind word and smile for everyone.

My most important dedication is to my partner in business, life and love, Terrie. She has lived with me through forty-three years of ups and downs in sports and business. I never had to question that she was in my corner, supporting me during the difficult times and kicking me in the ass whenever I felt sorry for myself. Terrie had a successful business career that she let take a backseat to my entrepreneurial route of building companies. She did so, however, in a calculating manner, first considering the financial outcome of my opportunities, which she determined could be greater than hers.

She taught me how to balance a checkbook, read a financial statement, deal with difficult customers and employees—and every freaking time I ignored her business advice, it came back to bite me. More than anything, whenever the *you-know-what* hit the fan, she always had my back.

Business and life are a lot like hockey. When you go into a game or confront any challenge, knowing that you have a teammate looking out for you makes it easier to face the world and be brave.

My entire life, I've not only been attracted to but—more importantly—I've been supported by strong, confident women. I'm especially grateful to have these three amazing, female role models and inspirations.

With love and appreciation,

Jerry

The close friends, family and people I have observed that have had a tremendous impact on my life:

Terrie Rollins	Clark Gillies
Bertha Rollins	Paddy Ginnell
Al Rollins	Marshall Goldsmith
Betty Jean Jones	Stephan Goss
Gary Anderson	Frank Greinke
Dr. Tony Baron	Steven Greinke
Scotty Bowman	Wayne Gretzky
Bear Bryant	Tony Hady
Stephen Covey	John Heffner
Raymond Crebs	Gordie Howe
Tom Deverell	Tony Hsieh
Dan Feder	Mark Howe
Jon Fehrman	Marty Howe
Stan Fischler	Bobby Hull
Terrell Fletcher	Ray Kroc
Jim Freeman	Eric Leitstein
Fred Galloway	Greg Lucier

Mark Messier

Jennifer Miller

Mike Moffett

Bill Murray

President Barack Obama

Dennis "Polo" Polonich

Jim Rohn

Red Scott

Sandra Sellani

Mr. Shalley

Lori Shaw-Cohen

Bradford D. Smart, PhD

Mr. Springenatic

Mr. Sturko

Jon Wampler

Jack Welch

Mr. Wells

Mr. Atamanchuk

John Wooden

CPSIA information can be obtained
at www.ICGtesting.com
Printed in the USA
LVHW010854300920
667476LV00004B/157

9 781949 635515